Statement Types

REM any text
REMARK any text

READ *variable*
READ *variable, . . . , variable*

LET *variable* = *expression*
GO TO *line number*

IF *expression*   *comparison*   *expression*   THEN *line number*

FOR *simple variable* = *expression* TO *expression* STEP *expression*
FOR *simple variable* = *expression* TO *expression*
NEXT *simple variable*

GOSUB *line number*
RETURN

PRINT
PRINT *expression*
PRINT *label*

$$\text{PRINT} \left\{ \begin{array}{c} label \\ or \\ expression \end{array} \right\}, \ldots, \left\{ \begin{array}{c} label \\ or \\ expression \end{array} \right\} \left\{ \begin{array}{c} , \\ or \\ blank \end{array} \right\}$$

DIM *letter* (*integer constant*)
DIM *letter* (*integer constant, integer constant*)

DATA *constant*
DATA *constant, . . . , constant*

STOP

functions

LOG	Natural logarithm
EXP	Exponential
ABS	Absolute value
SQR	Square root
INT	Integer part
SIN	Sine
COS	Cosine
TAN	Tangent
ATN	Arctangent
RND	Random number

BASIC

William F. Sharpe

University of Washington

BASIC An Introduction to Computer Programming Using the BASIC Language

New York THE FREE PRESS
London COLLIER-MACMILLAN LIMITED

Preface

Within the last few years the electronic digital computer has been transformed from a device understood only by members of a small cult of worshipers to an indispensable part of the life of every student, scientist, and businessman. Universities are now taking account of its importance with courses on computers, systems analysis, computer programming, and more esoteric aspects of a field rapidly becoming identified as computer science. Unfortunately an important market for information on computers is often overlooked when new courses are designed. A great many students in the social sciences, business administration, and even in the physical sciences wish to gain little more than a surface appreciation of computers; they simply want to use them in their academic work and understand enough about them to communicate with computer people in later life. Such students need not (and typically will not) learn enough about computers to instruct them in the languages designed for professional computer programmers (e.g., FORTRAN, COBOL, PL/I). Economical use of the time of such students (and that of faculty members) dictates that simple languages be utilized—sacrificing small amounts of relatively inexpensive

v

computer time in order to save major amounts of the user's time. This book provides an introduction to computer programming using such a language.

The language is BASIC, developed at Dartmouth College under the direction of Professor J. G. Kemeny. It has been implemented on most computers manufactured by the General Electric Company and is available on a commercial basis through the company's service bureaus. The Dartmouth and General Electric systems provide on-line capabilities—the user sits at a typewriter-like console and uses the computer as if it were his own, although in fact many others may be using it concurrently. However, the language can also be used in more conventional environments, with the user preparing his instructions and data on punched cards and submitting them for processing as part of a batch of such jobs at a central computer facility. To provide the use of the language in this manner a special programming system (UWBIC) has been prepared; it makes BASIC available to virtually anyone with access to a medium- or large-scale computer system.[1]

The language described in this book is a subset of the version of BASIC developed at Dartmouth for on-line use from teletypewriter consoles. A few minor changes are required if programs are to be keypunched for use with the UWBIC system, since the character set of the standard keypunch machine is more limited; such changes are described in footnotes to the text. Detailed information concerning the Dartmouth/GE system is given in Appendix A; Appendix B contains further information about the UWBIC system.

This book is designed to allow the user to think of a computer as if the latter "understands" the BASIC language. Thus no details of any of the supporting systems are included. This makes the book particularly suited for those unable to use a computer system, since it allows them to concentrate on the computational and logical properties of a high-level numerical computer language with relatively little concern for clerical details.

Very little is said about computers per se; the interested student is referred to any of the almost countless introductory texts or manuals on the subject.

BASIC is a simple but powerful language. The average college student should be able to learn it with five to ten hours of classroom exposure and an equal investment in time spent preparing actual programs. In many

1. The system will run on computers with a FORTRAN IV compiler, a word length of at least 32 bits, and core memory equivalent to at least 32,000 32-bit words. The system is described in W. F. Sharpe, *The University of Washington BASIC Interpretive Compiler*, Technical Reports Series No. 3, University of Washington Graduate School of Business Administration (Seattle, Washington). Copies of the system and the programs listed in Appendix C may be obtained from The Computer Software Management and Information Center, The University of Georgia, Athens, Georgia, for a nominal fee.

instances it may be both feasible and desirable to forgo some or all of the classroom time, relying instead on this book and the availability of helpful advice when the student encounters problems or questions. In the final analysis, the computer itself may be the best teacher.

WILLIAM F. SHARPE

Contents

BASIC

Chapter One

Introduction

The Computer and You

Imagine that you have a diligent, hard-working, and accurate, but totally unimaginative, assistant. Since she (he, it) is so unimaginative it is necessary for you to provide very precise sets of instructions (what to do) as well as data (what to do it to). In order to avoid any problems, you and the assistant have agreed upon a rather limited language—vocabulary and grammar—for stating your instructions. The language has the virtue that it admits no ambiguity. If you follow the rules when stating your desires, the assistant will do precisely what you have in mind. If any mistakes are made, they will necessarily be yours.

Now substitute computer for clerical assistant. Call the set of instructions a program. Call the language BASIC. Otherwise everything is the same.

The object of this book is to teach the grammar and vocabulary of BASIC. Although no computer actually "understands" BASIC directly, most medium- and large-scale machines can be taught (preconditioned) to act as if they do. The manner in which this takes place need not concern the reader; for all practical purposes one can assume that the computer understands BASIC.

1

Communication

To make the computer do your work, you must provide it with a *program* (indicating what to do), *data* (numbers to be processed), and certain information required to identify you, tell the computer how important you are, where to send the bill, and so forth. All of this must be sent to the computer somehow, and the computer must return information as well. Some installations provide users with typewriter-like consoles that can communicate directly with the computer. Others require that information be input from punched cards; output is then returned later, on printed sheets. Detailed information about such matters obviously must be obtained from those in charge of the installation to be utilized. This book deals with the more essential and more general aspects—the writing of programs and the arrangement of data.[1]

A program consists of a series of statements (instructions, or commands); each is written on a separate line. The lines are numbered from top to bottom, with smaller numbers preceding larger numbers. Systems that allow the user to enter lines from a typewriter-like console keep the lines in correct numeric sequence even if they are not entered in order. When using punched-card input, the user must usually arrange the cards correctly himself, with lower-numbered cards preceding higher-numbered cards.

Data are prepared in a similar fashion. Each line containing data is numbered, and the set of lines is arranged in sequence, either automatically (for typewriter entry systems) or by the user (for punched-card systems).

Nothing will be said here about operating teletypewriters, keypunch machines, and so on. Such information is easy to obtain; the best method is simply to spend five minutes at a machine with someone who knows how to operate it.

Diagnostic Messages

As we have suggested, you can assume that the computer recognizes instructions written in the BASIC language. But what if you present it with an illegal instruction (i.e., one that violates the rules for grammar and vocabulary presented in this manual)? In most cases the computer will be aware that it does not understand the instruction and make a reasonably well-informed guess about the source of its (more properly, your) confusion. And it will tell you about its difficulty and provide its diagnosis

---

1. Although some information about certain installations is given in Appendixes A and B.

of the problem. Don't be embarrassed by such *diagnostic messages;* most programmers learn more from them than from manuals.

Unfortunately the computer can only detect errors arising from illegal vocabulary and/or grammar; it cannot read your mind. If your program is constructed according to the rules, the computer will happily do precisely what you tell it to do. It is up to you to make certain that what you tell it to do is what you want it to do.

Output

When you submit a program and data to the computer, one or two operations take place. First, the computer looks over your program. If serious errors are found, it tells you about them (with alarming candor, on occasion), and then refuses to have anything more to do with you until you correct the errors. On the other hand, if it finds your program acceptable, it meekly begins to follow your instructions, looking at your data when told to do so and providing answers in accordance with your instructions.

Chapter Two

Getting Started

Here is an extremely simple program:

```
10    REMARK -- PAYROLL PROGRAM

20    REMARK -- PROGRAMMER, LYNDON B. JOHNSON

30    READ P
35    READ H

45    LET G = P * H
60    LET W = .14 * G
70    LET N = G - W

80    PRINT P
90    PRINT H
100   PRINT G
110   PRINT W
120   PRINT N

140   GO TO 30
```

A set of data to go with it might look like this:

5

```
900   DATA  1.25
901   DATA 40
902   DATA  2.00
903   DATA 41
904   DATA  1.97
905   DATA 35
906   DATA  2.10
907   DATA 49
```

Format

To make a program easy to read we often insert spaces, indent some statements, include blank lines, and so on. None of this has any effect on the program; write it any way you choose. You might as well get used to capital letters; there are no lower-case letters on most input devices. Blanks may be inserted as desired; with one exception (described in Chapter 4), they have no effect on the meaning of a statement.

Line Numbers

Note that each statement in the program has a line number and that the numbers are arranged in order. This is required in most installations.[1] Line numbers must be between 1 and 99999[2] (but only integers—whole numbers—are allowed). It is a good idea to leave gaps when assigning numbers (e.g., writing 10, 20, 30, and so on) in case you subsequently wish to insert additional statements.

Remarks

Every statement must begin with a legal command (after the line number, if any). The first two commands in this program are remarks. A remark is used to provide information for you and/or anyone else reading your program; it provides no information to the computer. In fact, the computer ignores remarks (saying, in effect, "He is only talking to himself, not to me"). To indicate a remark, simply use the command REM; after that you may write anything you please.

---

1. If the installation uses the UWBIC system, however, line numbers are optional and need not be arranged in order; only the position of the card in the deck is relevant.

2. With UWBIC, line numbers must be between 1 and 9999.

Instruction Sequence

A program is nothing more than a set of instructions (although remarks are instructions only in a rather academic sense). The computer is expected to follow the instructions in order (from the top of the page to the bottom), unless told to do otherwise.

Variables

The computer is provided with a number of "mailboxes," each of which can hold a number. Each mailbox has a name. There are twenty-six mailboxes with simple one-letter names: A, B, C, . . . Z. The remaining mailboxes have two-character names—a letter followed by a digit: A0, A1, . . . A9, B0, . . . B9, C0, . . . Z9.

For convenience, we often use the name of a mailbox to indicate the number in it. And since the number in a mailbox may be taken out and a new one put in its place we often refer to the number in a mailbox as a *variable* (since it may vary as the program is executed). Thus variable A means the number currently in mailbox A, variable B3 means the number currently in mailbox B3.

Reading Data

The data to be operated on by a program consists of a set of numbers. It is useful to think of the numbers as if they were in a stack similar to that used for dishes in many restaurants. At any given time there is a number at the top of the stack; when it is used (read) the next one pops up to the top of the stack.

The numbers are loaded into the data stack from the DATA statements *before* the computer begins to follow the programmed instructions. In this case, the number 1.25 will be at the top of the stack, the number 40 will be next, and so on.

We are now in a position to understand statement 30 in the program. It says, "Take the number from the top of the data stack and put it in mailbox P, throwing away any number that might be there already." Thus after statement 30 has been executed the first time, the number 1.25 will be in mailbox P (and the number 40 will be at the top of the data stack).

What happens when the computer encounters statement 35? The number from the top of the stack (40) is placed in mailbox H and 2.00 pops up to the top of the stack.

We often describe this process in more elegant terms. For example, we might say that the *value* 1.25 has been *assigned to* variable P. Or, more explicitly, we might say that 1.25 has been *read into* P. In any event, the process is clear enough.

It should come as no surprise that P is being used to represent the hourly pay rate of some employee and H the number of hours he worked during the week. The object of the program is to compute his gross pay (G), withholding (W), and net pay (N). The computations are performed as specified by instructions 45, 60, and 70.

Expressions

Look at statement 45. The portion to the right of the equal sign is an *expression*. It specifies that certain *computations* are to be performed and a *value* obtained. To be specific, P * H says, "Multiply the number currently in mailbox P by the number currently in mailbox H; the result is the *value of the expression*." Note that the numbers in P and H are *not* altered when the expression is evaluated.

Expressions are formed according to the standard rules of arithmetic. Five basic operations are available:[3]

+ Addition
− Subtraction
* Multiplication
/ Division
↑ Exponentiation

Certain problems present themselves, however. Since the entire expression must be written on one line, ambiguities may arise. To divide A by the sum of B and C, you might say:

$$A/B + C$$

But this might be interpreted by the computer as the sum of A/B and C. It is possible to find out the rules the computer uses when there is an ambiguity, but why bother? Instead, just uses parentheses to avoid any problems:

$$A/(B + C)$$

Expressions may be very complicated:

$$(C ** (A3/(B * X))) - Z5$$

or very simple:

$$X4$$

---

3. With UWBIC, a double asterisk (**) is used instead of the arrow (↑) to indicate exponentiation.

They may use variables and/or *constants*. A constant is simply a number written in the program. The rules for writing numbers apply to both constants and numbers included as data:

1. A decimal point may or may not be included.
2. A minus number is indicated by preceding the number with a minus sign.
3. A positive number need not be preceded by a plus sign.
4. Commas may *not* be included.

Some legal numbers are:

$$.01$$
$$.3$$
$$256.4$$
$$35$$
$$-1.2$$

To summarize, an expression may be

1. A variable or
2. A constant or
3. Any combination of variables and/or constants connected by operators, with parentheses included when necessary to avoid ambiguity

When an expression is evaluated, the current values of the variables (if any) are used, along with the constants (if any) to obtain a single value (number). The values of the variables are *not* altered when the expression is evaluated.

LET Commands

The form of a LET command is

LET *variable* = *expression*

It says, simply,

1. Evaluate the expression on the right-hand side of the equal sign
2. Then insert that value in the mailbox (variable) indicated on the left-hand side of the equal sign, throwing away any value currently in the mailbox

When the program reaches statement 45 for the first time, the current value of P (1.25) will be multiplied by H (40). The result (50) will then be placed in box G. The values of P and H are, of course, unchanged. After statement 45 has been executed, G will contain the gross pay for the individual being processed.

Statement 60 uses the value of G for further computation. It instructs the computer to multiply the current value of G (50) by .14; the result (7) is then placed in box W. This is obviously the amount to be withheld.

Statement 70 calculates the individual's net pay (G − W) and inserts it in box N. The calculations are now complete.

PRINT Commands

It does little good to perform calculations if the results are simply left in the computer where no one can see them. Thus we instruct the computer:

80   PRINT P

This means, simply, "Print the number in box P." Printing has no effect on the contents of the boxes, it merely allows the user to see what the contents are. The full set of instructions:

80   PRINT P
90   PRINT H
100   PRINT G
110   PRINT W
120   PRINT N

causes the following numbers to be printed:

1.25
40
50
7
43

Needless to say, this is hardly very elegant output. We will learn how to improve it later; for the present be content with the ability to get numbers out of the computer and onto the output sheet where you can see them.

GO TO Commands

Although it is comforting to know that the computer has accurately processed the payroll for the first employee (the one making $1.25 per hour), it would hardly be worthwhile to write a program to do so little work. Had we wanted no more from the computer, we could have said:

140 STOP

But there are other employees to be processed; we want to tell the computer to do to them what it did to the first employee. To do this we simply instruct it to alter the normal sequence in which it follows instructions:

140 GO TO 30

This says, simply, "Go back to statement 30, then proceed again in order until I tell you to do otherwise."

What happens? The computer encounters statement 30, which instructs it to read the number at the top of the data stack (2.00) into location (variable, or mailbox) P; the former value (1.25) is thrown away in the process. The next statement instructs the computer to read the next data number (41) into H, and its former value is thrown away in the process. Then the computations are performed using the *current* values of P and H. Obviously the resulting values of G, W, and N will be those applicable to the new employee. For example, when statement 45 is executed, P * H (2.00 * 41) will be placed in G and the former value thrown away. Thus G will equal 82—the second employee's gross pay for the week. W and N will be computed similarly. And the final results (including P and H, shown for the record) will be printed on the output sheet.

After the second employee's payroll has been printed, the computer will again reach statement 140 and will once again go back to statement 30. The third employee's pay will be processed, then the fourth, then the fifth, and so on. When will it all stop? When the computer runs out of numbers. Obviously no more can then be done for you, so the computer will turn to someone else's job.

Reprise

For all its simplicity, the program shown here could be used to compute gross pay, withholding, and net pay accurately and rapidly for a great many (thousands, if you wish) employees. Every week you could prepare a new set of data and get a completely different set of results using the same program. Needless to say, there is more to the BASIC language; you will soon be able to do many more things (and to do them more elegantly). But it is useful to learn to crawl before attempting to run. Try to answer the problems at the end of this chapter (if you can't, reread the material before looking at the answers provided). Then write some programs of your own using the portions of the language you now know. The computer will help you.

Problems

1. Find any errors in the following expressions:

> (a) 3
> (b) X
> (c) A0 + B3
> (d) AB/C
> (e) A + (B/C) * D
> (f) −3 + X
> (g) (8 + Z2)/−6
> (h) A35 + C
> (i) 3X/D
> (j) (Q + I)W9
> (k) ((A + B)/(C − X) ↑ 8
> (l) 3 * (A/+8)
> (m) A ↑ .5

2. What output would be produced if the set of data given for the payroll program (at the beginning of this chapter) were submitted with the following program?

```
  5     READ X
 10     READ Y
 15     READ Z
 20     READ Z2

100     PRINT X
105     PRINT Y
110     LET Q0 = X*Y
115     PRINT Q0
120     LET Q0 = Z2 - Z
125     PRINT Q0

150     GO TO 5
```

3. The value of a dollar at the end of N years compounded annually at an interest rate of 10 percent per year is:

$$\text{value} = 1.10 \uparrow N$$

Write a program to read a set of values of N, producing for each one the value of a dollar at the end of that many years. Be certain to print N each time.

4. Write a complete program to do some sort of calculation, and prepare at least a few lines of data to test the program. When preparing your program—

(a) Follow the sample program in this chapter fairly closely.
(b) Limit your computations to relatively simple combinations of basic operations, using parentheses whenever there might be any ambiguity concerning your intentions.
(c) Be certain that your program will terminate, either by reaching a STOP statement or by running out of data.
(d) Try not to be too ambitious the first time. You may want to build confidence by merely copying the sample program and adding one or two extra computations and outputs.
(e) If your program will not run, read the diagnostic messages from the computer, make the necessary corrections, and try again.
(f) If the program runs but produces incorrect answers, play computer: follow your own instructions until you find the error in your logic. Then correct the program and try again.

Answers

1.

(a) This is perfectly legal; a constant is a valid expression.
(b) This is legal, too; a variable is a valid expression.
(c) This is legal; A0 is a valid variable name, as is B3. The value of this expression will be the sum of the numbers currently in boxes A0 and B3.
(d) Illegal. A is a variable name, as is B. If the programmer had meant to multiply A times B, he should have said so:

$$(A * B)/C$$

If the programmer thought that AB was a valid variable name, he needs to reread the chapter.
(e) This is perfectly legal; however, it is ambiguous. To make absolutely certain the computer will do what you want it to do, you should add some more parentheses, e.g.:

$$(A + (B/C)) * D$$

If you want to know what the computer will in fact do when there is ambiguity, the rules are

    (1) Expressions inside parentheses are evaluated first;
    (2) Within a set of parentheses,
        a) all exponentiation (↑) is performed first, from left to right;
        b) multiplications (*) and divisions (/) are performed next, from left to right;
        c) additions (+) and subtractions (−) are performed last, from left to right.

(f) This is legal; −3 is treated as a constant.

(g) This may or may not be legal, depending on the system used. The constant −6 conforms to the rules; however, the fact that the division operator (/) is next to the minus sign may cause a diagnostic message, since a minus sign is also used to indicate subtraction. To avoid such a possibility it is a good idea to throw in extra parentheses:

$$(8 + Z2)/(-6)$$

The general rule is to avoid situations in which two operators are next to each other.

(h) This is illegal. A35 is not a valid variable name. The computer will probably think that you have put a variable (A3) next to a constant (5). Whatever the computer thinks it has found, it won't like it.

(i) This is illegal, too. If the programmer meant 3 times X, he should have said so:

$$(3 * X)/D$$

(j) Same problem. Multiplication must be indicated explicitly:

$$(Q + I) * W9$$

(k) The parentheses fail to pair up here. To avoid this kind of error it is useful to check complicated expressions, using the following scheme. Read the expression from left to right, keeping a cumulative count. Start the count at 0. Whenever you find a left parenthesis—(—add one to the count. Whenever you find a right parenthesis—)—subtract one. The count should never become negative and should be zero when you reach the end of the expression. If not, you have made a mistake. If you don't find it, the computer will.

(1) As in (g), this expression may or may not be legal, depending on the system used, since the computer may be confused by the two adjacent operators. To cure this, drop the plus sign, because it is redundant:

$$3 * (A/8)$$

(m) Perfectly legal. The value of this expression will be the square root of A.

2.
$$
\begin{array}{c}
1.25 \\
40 \\
50 \\
39 \\
1.97 \\
35 \\
68.95 \\
46.90
\end{array}
$$

3. There are, of course, many ways to write a program designed to accomplish any given task. The important point is to write one that works (whether or not it is "efficient" is clearly a secondary matter). A program to compute the values specified for this problem follows:

```
10    READ N
20    PRINT N
30    LET V = 1.10↑N
40    PRINT V
50    GO TO 10
```

4. Good luck.

Chapter Three

Conditional Transfers

The program in Chapter 2 was fine for determining pay and withholding for each individual on the payroll. Reduced to its fundamentals, the program looked like that shown in Figure 3.1, page 18.

This is a classic example of a *loop*—the main reason that it pays people to write computer programs. In essence we told the computer what to do for the first man on the payroll and then instructed it to loop back, read new data, repeat the computations, print the results, loop back, and so forth. The computer gets out of this loop by following the sensible rule that whenever it runs out of data there is nothing to do but give up.

The IF-THEN Command

You may not want the machine to merely stop after reading all the payroll data. Perhaps you would like to have it finish with a summary of the number of persons paid, total amount paid, and total amount withheld. To do this you need a *conditional transfer*—a statement that tells the computer to go (transfer) somewhere if (but only if) a certain condition is met.

Remember the way in which we set up the payroll data—each man's hourly pay rate was followed by the number of hours he worked during the week. After processing each man, the computer returned to process

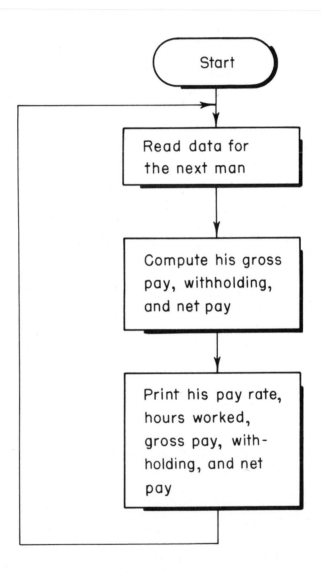

Figure 3.1

the next one. Our problem is to find some way to tell it when all the people have been processed. One way to do this is to simply add an unusual man at the end—one with an hourly rate of, say, —1 per hour, who worked, say, —40 hours. Knowing that such a man will be the last in the set of data, we can instruct the computer to watch out for him and to transfer to a set of instructions for preparing summary information when it encounters him.

The new arrangement is shown in Figure 3.2 on page 20.

After reading each pair of numbers, we tell the computer to look at the number it put in box P. If it is not negative, the numbers referred to a real man and are to be processed accordingly. But if the number read into box P was negative, the numbers did not refer to a real man; they were a signal to indicate that the last man has already been processed. When this condition takes place we want the computer to transfer out of the loop and print the desired summary information.

The new program follows:

```
10      REMARK -- A MORE IMPRESSIVE PAYROLL PROGRAM
11      REMARK -- PROGRAMMER, DAN EVANS

20      REMARK -- GET READY FOR PROCESSING
21         LET N0 = 0
22         LET T1 = 0
23         LET T2 = 0

30      REMARK -- READ DATA FOR THE NEXT MAN
31         READ P
32         READ H

40      REMARK -- TEST FOR COMPLETION
41         IF P < 0 THEN 100

50      REMARK -- COMPUTE THIS MANS PAYROLL
51         LET G = P * H
52         LET W = .14 * G
53         LET N = G - W

60      REMARK -- PRINT HIS PAYROLL
61         PRINT P
62         PRINT H
63         PRINT G
64         PRINT W
65         PRINT N
```

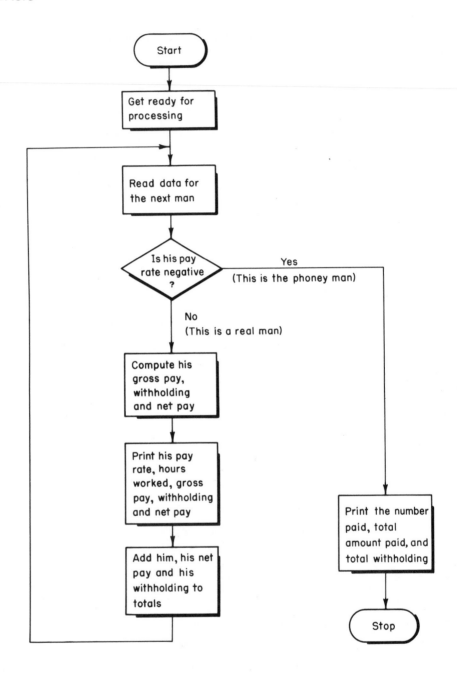

Figure 3.2

```
 70     REMARK -- ADD HIM, HIS PAY AND WITHHLDG TO TOTALS
 71        LET NO = NO + 1
 72        LET 11 = T1 + N
 73        LET 12 = T2 + W

 80     REMARK -- GO BACK TO READ MORE DATA
 81        GO TO 30

100     REMARK -- THIS POINT REACHED WHEN ALL MEN PROCESSED

101     REMARK -- PRINT NUMBER PAID, TOTAL PAID AND WITHLDG
102        PRINT NO
103        PRINT T1
104        PRINT T2

110     STOP
```

The conditional transfer in the program is:

41   IF P < O THEN 100

Its meaning is

> "If the current value of (number in the box named) P is less than ($<$) zero, then go to line number 100. If it is not, proceed to the line that follows this statement (i.e., number 50)."

In general, a condition compares the values of two expressions. Of course either expression may be simply a variable or a constant. Six types of comparison are possible:[1]

Comparison	Read as
$>$	"is greater than"
$<$	"is less than"
$=$	"is equal to"
$> =$	"is greater than or equal to"
$< =$	"is less than or equal to"
$< >$	"is less than or greater than" / "is not equal to"

The following examples illustrate the way in which the conditional

---

[1] With UWBIC, the comparisons are:

Comparison	Read as
GT	"is greater than"
LT	"is less than"
$=$	"is equal to"
GE	"is greater than or equal to"
LE	"is less than or equal to"
NE	"is not equal to" / "is less than or greater than"

transfer is used:

Statement	Meaning
IF A = G THEN 193	If the current value of A is equal to the current value of G, go to line number 193. If not, proceed.
IF A < > G THEN 503	If the current value of A does not equal the current value of G, go to line number 503. If it does, proceed.
IF N > 100 THEN 324	If the current value of N is greater than 100, go to line number 324. If it is not (i.e., it is less than or equal to 100), proceed.
IF N > = 100 THEN 433	If the current value of N is greater than or equal to 100, go to line number 433. If it is not (i.e., it is less than 100), proceed.
IF W < 5 THEN 234	If the current value of W is less than 5, go to line number 234. If it is not (i.e., it is greater than or equal to 5), proceed.
IF W < = 5 THEN 235	If the current value of W is less than or equal to 5, go to line number 235. If it is not (i.e., it is greater than 5), proceed.

The quantities to be compared may be very complicated expressions. But (as always) be certain to use parentheses whenever there might be any ambiguity. For example:

$$\text{IF } A > B - C \text{ THEN } 500$$
$$\text{IF } (3 * A) - (B \uparrow 2) = Q \uparrow 8 \text{ THEN } 300$$
$$\text{IF } (8 - C) * B < 34 \text{ THEN } 200$$

The New Program

Initialization

Before the first man's payroll is processed, the number of personnel paid (to be recorded in box N0), the total amount paid out (to be recorded in box T1), and the total amount withheld (to be recorded in box T2) should all be zero. Statements 21, 22, and 23 set these variables to their initial values (zero). Statement 21, for example, says, "Put the number 0 in box N0." Most loops are preceded by one or more such *initialization* instructions.

Reading the Data

The READ statements are similar to those in the earlier program. The first time through the loop, the first two numbers from the data stack are read; the second time through, the next two are read; and so on.

Conditional Transfer

This is our new statement. If the numbers just read included a negative pay rate, the computer is supposed to go to line number 100. If not, it proceeds (to line number 50).

Computing and Printing Pay and Withholding

If the computer has read real payroll data into P and H, it will not transfer to statement 100 when it looks at P. Instead, it will proceed to compute the man's pay and withholding and print the results. The required statements (50 through 53 and 60 through 65) are, of course, similar to those used in the first payroll program.

Adding to Totals

After computing the pay and withholding for a new man, we want to record the fact that we have paid one more person. To do this we write:

$$71 \quad \text{LET } N0 = N0 + 1$$

In essence this says:

> "Take the number currently in box N0, add one to it, then put the result in box N0 (throwing out the previous value)."

Obviously N0 is serving as a *counter*—every time a new man's pay is processed, N0 is increased (or stepped up) by one. When the last pair of numbers is reached and the computer transfers to statement 100, N0 will equal the total number of people paid.

The other instructions keep the cumulative sums of pay and withholding. The statement,

$$72 \quad \text{LET } T1 = T1 + N$$

says:

> "Take the number currently in box T1, add to it this man's net pay (N) and put the results in box T1 (throwing out the previous value)."

When the last pair of numbers is reached and the computer transfers to statement 100, T1 will equal the total amount paid out.

The third statement (73) takes care of withholding; when statement 100 is reached, T2 will equal the sum of the amounts withheld.

Printing Summary Information

The section of the program starting with statement 100 is reached only after a negative pay rate is read. The next three statements (102, 103, and 104) print the desired summary information. Since no more work remains to be done, we tell the computer to STOP.

Style

Some additional points are worth mentioning before leaving this example. First, notice the many remarks used to remind the reader of the programmer's intentions. If anything, there are too few remarks here. Good practice would dictate that the programmer identify the meaning attached to various key variables. For example:

$$15 \quad \text{REMARK---P} = \text{PAY RATE IN DOLLARS PER HOUR}$$

Notice also the number of blank lines used to set off different sections of the program. Finally, notice that some statements have been indented to help show the relationships among groups of instructions. Inasmuch as the computer generally ignores blanks, this does not affect the operation of the program, and it may help considerably when you (or someone else) try to reconstruct the logic.

These are good habits. They require relatively little time when you are writing a program, and they may save a great deal of time later on.

Multiple Conditions

We have seen that the conditional transfer can be used to branch to a desired point in the program if some condition is met. But you may want to branch if any one of *several* conditions is met. Assume that a special procedure is required for employees with more than two dependents or with a gross pay exceeding $200 per week. If this special procedure begins at line number 300, the program could include the following statements:

$$100 \quad \text{IF} \ D > 2 \ \text{THEN} \ 300$$
$$101 \quad \text{IF} \ G > 200 \ \text{THEN} \ 300$$

Obviously a number of other conditions could be added. If any were met, the computer would transfer to line number 300. If none was met, it would proceed to the next statement (i.e., the one following the last IF statement).

Take another case. Assume that a procedure is to be followed if (and only if) a number of conditions are met. For example, the amount to be withheld might be zero if an employee had *more than* three dependents *and* earned *under* $100 per week. If both conditions are not met, some alternative procedure beginning with line number 250 is to be followed. This situation can be represented in a manner similar to that shown in the previous example:

$$201 \quad \text{IF } D <= 3 \text{ THEN } 250$$
$$202 \quad \text{IF } G >= 100 \text{ THEN } 250$$
$$203 \quad \text{LET } W = 0$$

By carefully arranging conditional transfers, you can represent virtually any type of multiple condition. As always, it pays to check the logic by playing computer, following your instructions with test data to insure that they do what you want them to do.

Problems

1.   What is wrong with this set of instructions?

```
100     IF G < 200 THEN 120
110     LET T = .14 * G
120     LET T = 0
130     LET N = G - T
```

2.   The computer is in the midst of a program. At the moment, the current values of key variables are

A	3.5
B3	−5.6
Z	100.2
Q2	0
F	1
K	−4.2
T9	100.2

For each of the following statements, decide whether or not the computer will transfer to statement 500:

(a) IF A > F THEN 500
(b) IF A < F THEN 500
(c) IF B3 < K THEN 500
(d) IF Z < T9 THEN 500
(e) IF Z <= T9 THEN 500
(f) IF Q2 > 3.2 THEN 500

3. The rules actually followed when computing the amount to be withheld for federal income tax are rather involved. The amount to be withheld depends on (a) whether the taxpayer is single or married; (b) the number of exemptions he has claimed; and (c) the amount he earns. Assume that the data to be processed include the following information for each employee (in the order specified): (a) his hourly pay rate; (b) the number of hours worked during the last *two* weeks; (c) the digit 0 (if he is single) or the digit 1 (if he is married); and (d) the number of exemptions he has claimed. The following tables indicate the rules used by a typical firm:

Single Persons—Including Heads of Household

If the amount of wages during a two-week period (after allowing $29.20 for each claimed exemption) is

The amount of income tax to be withheld shall be

Not over $8   0

Over	But not over		of excess over
$8	$29	14%	$8
$29	$50	$2.94, plus 15%	$29
$50	$183	$6.09, plus 17%	$50
$183	$367	$28.70, plus 20%	$183
$367	$458	$65.50, plus 25%	$367
$458		$88.25, plus 30%	$458

Married Persons

If the amount of wages during a two-week period (after allowing $29.20 for each claimed exemption) is

The amount of income tax to be withheld shall be

Not over $8   0

Over	But not over		of excess over
$8	$50	14%	$8
$50	$183	$5.88, plus 15%	$50
$183	$367	$25.83, plus 17%	$183
$367	$738	$57.11, plus 20%	$367
$738	$917	$131.31, plus 25%	$738
$917		$176.06, plus 30%	$917

Write a program to read the information on each employee and compute the amount to be withheld from his income for the two-week period.

4. Make up some data to go with the program you wrote when answering

problem 3. Be sure to include at least one person falling in each of the categories indicated in the rules for withholding. Then run your program and check its results with hand computations. This will prove to be time-consuming but it constitutes an acid test of your program. It will also give you a real appreciation for the power of the computer (and the advantages derived from being able to program it).

5. Now program something that interests you. Be certain that your program will terminate by either reaching a STOP statement or running out of data. Run the program with real or test data. And keep at it until the program really works.

Answers

1. Presumably the programmer wants to let T equal 0 if G is less than 200, and to let T equal .14 * G otherwise. The first goal is clearly met, but the second is not. To see why, assume that G is greater than 200. The condition in statement 100 is not met, so the computer proceeds to statement 110, which sets T equal to .14 * G. So far so good. But then the computer goes on to statement 120 which tosses out the current (desired) value of T and puts zero in instead. Obviously the computer should be told to skip statement 120 in this case. A solution to the problem follows:

```
100     IF G < 200 THEN 120
110     LET T = .14 * G
115     GO TO 130
120     LET T = 0
130     LET N = G - T
```

2.
    (a) 3.5 is greater than 1; the computer will transfer to statement 500.
    (b) 3.5 is not less than 1; the computer will not transfer to statement 500.
    (c) −5.6 is less than −4.2; the computer will transfer to statement 500. Think of numbers as lying along a scale:

$$-5.6 \qquad\qquad -4.2 \qquad\qquad 0 \qquad\qquad +5$$

If one number lies to the right of another, we say it is greater; if it lies to the left, we say it is smaller.

(d) 100.2 is not less than 100.2; thus the computer will not transfer to statement 500.

(e) 100.2 is not less than 100.2, but it is equal to it; as long as either of the conditions is met, the computer will transfer to statement 500.

(f) Zero is not greater than 3.2; the computer will not transfer to statement 500.

3. There are many possible ways to program this. The version shown below is just one of them. After data for an employee are read (statements 10 through 13), his gross pay (G) and taxable income (T) are computed. These computations are required for all employees and are thus performed first. Next the employee's taxable income is checked to see if it exceeds $8.00 (statement 26). If not, his withholding is set to zero and the computer is instructed to go directly to the section for final processing (beginning with statement 200). If taxable income does exceed $8.00, the computer is told to see if the employee is married or not (statement 31). If the employee is married, processing begins with statement 100; if not, processing begins with statement 40. In either case the income bracket is found by *successively checking to see if T is less than increasingly larger* amounts. To see why this works, consider a single employee with gross income of $100. The computer will not transfer to statement 50 when it follows the instruction at statement 41. The mere fact that statement 42 is reached thus guarantees that his income exceeds $29. But if his income is not less than or equal to $50, the computer will proceed to statement 43. The fact that statement 43 is reached indicates that the employee is single and has an income greater than $50. If his income is also less than $183 (as we assume it is in this case), the computer will transfer to statement 70, which indicates the relevant amount to be withheld. Then the computer is told to transfer to the final portion of the program (located at statement 200).

The general procedure for finding the appropriate amount to be withheld is to pass through a number of IF statements involving less and less stringent requirements. When the appropriate bracket is found the condition will be met and the computer will transfer to the relevant instruction. If none of the tests is met (e.g., if the employee is single and earns over $458), the statement following the last IF statement will be reached.

The final section of this program simply computes the employee's net pay, prints the results, and then transfers back to process a new employee. These operations are the same for all employees and are thus written just once.

```
  1    REMARK -- WITHHOLDING PROGRAM


  5    REMARK -- READ DATA
 10       READ P
 11       READ H
 12       READ M
 13       READ E

 20    REMARK -- COMPUTE GROSS PAY AND TAXABLE INCOME
 21       LET G = P * H
 22       LET T = G - ( 29.20 * E )

 25    REMARK -- SEE WHETHER TAXABLE INCOME EXCEEDS 8 DOL
 26    IF T > 8 THEN 30
 27       REMARK -- NO WITHHOLDING REQUIRED
 28       LET W = 0
 29       GO TO 200

 30    REMARK -- WITHHOLDING REQUIRED, SEE IF MARRIED
 31    IF M = 1 THEN 100

 40    REMARK -- EMPLOYEE IS SINGLE, FIND BRACKET
 41    IF T <= 29 THEN 50
 42    IF T <= 50 THEN 60
 43    IF T <= 183 THEN 70
 44    IF T <= 367 THEN 80
 45    IF T <= 458 THEN 90
 46    LET W = 88.25 + ( .30 * (T-458) )
 47    GO TO 200
 50    LET W = .14 * (T-8)
 51    GO TO 200
 60    LET W = 2.94 + ( .15 * (T-29) )
 61    GO TO 200
 70    LET W = 6.09 + ( .17 * (T-50) )
 71    GO TO 200
 80    LET W = 28.70 + ( .20 * (T-183) )
 81    GO TO 200
 90    LET W = 65.50 + ( .25 * (T-367) )
 91    GO TO 200

100    REMARK -- EMPLOYEE IS MARRIED, CHECK BRACKET
101    IF T <= 50 THEN 110
102    IF T <= 183 THEN 120
103    IF T <= 367 THEN 130
104    IF T <= 738 THEN 140
105    IF T <= 917 THEN 150
```

```
106     LET W = 176.06 + ( .30 * (T-917) )
107     GO TO 200
110     LET W = .14 * (T-8)
111     GO TO 200
120     LET W = 5.88 + ( .15 * (T-50) )
121     GO TO 200
130     LET W = 25.83 + ( .17 * (T-183) )
131     GO TO 200
140     LET W = 57.11 + ( .20 * (T-367) )
141     GO TO 200
150     LET W = 131.31 + ( .25 * (T-738) )

200     REMARK -- COMPUTE NET PAY AND PRINT RESULTS
201     LET N = G - W
202     PRINT P
203     PRINT H
204     PRINT G
205     PRINT W
206     PRINT N

210     REMARK -- RETURN TO PROCESS THE NEXT MAN
211     GO TO 5
```

4. Good luck.

5. See the answer to problem 4.

Chapter Four

Reading and Printing

By now you should be able to do rather esoteric types of computations; but the way you get data into the computer and, more importantly, the form in which you get answers from the computer are likely to cause you some embarrassment. This chapter will expand your ability to control such operations. Although you will not be able to do things as elegantly as a professional might, you will be able to use convenient forms of input and to produce readable output.

Data

As we have seen, you can think of data numbers as if they were in a stack similar to that used for dishes—when the top one is removed (by a READ statement), the next one pops up to the top. To make this arrangement as vivid as possible we have included just one number in each DATA statement. But this is not necessary at all. You may include as many numbers as you wish; just separate them with commas. The stack will be filled by reading the first DATA statement from left to right, then the second, then the third, and so forth.

For example:

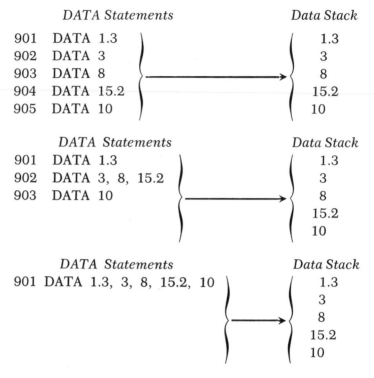

	DATA Statements		Data Stack
901	DATA 1.3		1.3
902	DATA 3		3
903	DATA 8		8
904	DATA 15.2		15.2
905	DATA 10		10

Obviously the way in which the user writes any given set of numbers is primarily a matter of convenience. However they are written, the numbers (and only the numbers) will be put in the data stack in the order of their appearance (reading each DATA statement from left to right and all statements in order). Of course only the data stack is relevant when the program goes to work.

DATA statements may be interspersed with program statements. However, to avoid confusion it is best to write them as a group after the last statement in the program.

READ Commands

Recall the way we have been writing READ commands:

READ P

This means "Take the number from the top of the data stack and put it in box P." To read two numbers in sequence we have said:

READ P
READ H

This is clearly a bother. The same thing can be accomplished by merely saying:

READ P, H

Would you like to read three values? Simply say:

READ X1, Y, Z9

This is precisely equivalent to

READ X1
READ Y
READ Z9

You need only separate the names of the relevant variables with commas (so the computer will not get confused). Numbers from the data stack will be put in the boxes indicated (from left to right).

Often it is useful to coordinate READ statements and DATA statements. You might choose to put each employee's data in a single DATA statement:

DATA 2.10, 41, 1, 2

and read it with the statement:

READ P, H, M, E

But remember that the correspondence is strictly for your benefit. Any equivalent arrangement of READ statements and/or DATA statements would give the same results.

Labels

A label is anything you would like to have printed (except quotation marks) enclosed in quotation marks.[1] Labels are used to print a message as part of the output. For example:

PRINT "PAYROLL FOR JUNE, 1967"

The label will be printed exactly as you have written it, except that the quotation marks will not appear. This means that blanks *do* count in labels. In fact, this is the only place in a BASIC program where blanks are at all relevant.

Skipping Lines

Output produced with BASIC is single-spaced. If you wish, however,

---

1. UWBIC uses the apostrophe (') instead of a quotation mark (").

you may tell the computer to skip a line.[2] To do this, simply tell it to print nothing:

PRINT

Printing the Values of Expressions

Thus far we have only asked the computer to print the values of variables. For example:

PRINT P

But you may ask for the value of any legal expression:

PRINT P
PRINT 3.5
PRINT A + 8
PRINT (X * 3) ↑ 8

The expression will be evaluated, then the value (number) will be printed. The computer will decide the best way to print it. Generally the number will be rounded to six significant digits (i.e., the left-most digit that is not zero and the five digits to its right), and then printed in a reasonably attractive manner.[3] If the number is extremely large or extremely small the computer may be forced to print it as a decimal fraction followed by E and an appropriate power of ten. Of course none of this affects the values of numbers in the computer (i.e., in the locations)—they remain in their original state.

Print Zones

The output sheet is divided into five zones, each fifteen columns wide. Think of the computer as if it were a typewriter with tab stops every fifteen columns. Now, look at the following command:

PRINT P, H, M, E

This says: print the value of P (in the first zone), then tab and print the value of H (in the second zone), then tab and print the value of M (in the third zone), and finally, tab and print the value of E (in the fourth zone).

---

2. With UWBIC, you may also tell it to go to the top of a new page. The command is simply:

PAGE

3. Dartmouth/GE systems print numbers beginning in the left-most column of a zone (see the following section); the UWBIC system centers numbers within zones.

Notice that the commas can be regarded as instructions to "Hit the tab key."

What if the computer runs out of zones, as in:

PRINT P, H, M, E, X1, X2

The answer is obvious: X2 will be printed in the first zone on the next line.

Remember that you can ask the computer to print the value of any expression. For example, an entire payroll program might be written as follows:

```
10    READ P, H
20    PRINT P, H, P*H,    .14*(P*H),   .86*(P*H)
30    GO TO 10
```

You may also include labels. They are printed starting at the beginning of the next available zone. If a label requires more than fifteen columns it will, of course, occupy more than one zone.

The output of the payroll program shown above could be improved using labels:

```
6    PRINT "PAY RATE","HOURS","GROSS","WITHHLDG","NET"
7    PRINT

10   READ P, H
20   PRINT P, H, P*H,   .14*(P*H),   .86*(P*H)
30   GO TO 10
```

You can, of course, print both labels and numeric values on the same line. For example:

PRINT "PAY RATE = ", P

would produce this sort of output:

PAY RATE = 2.15

The Dangling Comma

Normally the output generated by a PRINT command is begun in the first zone of a new line. There is one exception, however. If the previously executed PRINT command *ended* with a comma, the new output is started in the next available zone. Thus the two programs below produce equivalent output:

Program A:

```
10      READ P, H
20      LET G = P * H
30      LET W = .14 * G
40      LET N = G - W
50      PRINT P, H, G, W, N
60      GO TO 10
```

Program B:

```
100     READ P, H
110     PRINT P, H,
120     LET G = P * H
130     PRINT G,
140     LET W = .14 * G
150     PRINT W,
160     LET N = G - W
170     PRINT N
180     GO TO 100
```

Problems

1. Find any errors in the following statements:

   (a) PRINT "NUMBER EARNING "BREAD" REGULARLY"
   (b) PRINT A + B, C, "X =, X"
   (c) PRINT 3, 5.8, 9
   (d) READ A, B, C + D
   (e) READ A, B,

2. Write a command that will print the word HELLO in the second zone.

3. Write a statement to print the letter X in the center of zone one.

4. What output would be produced by the following program and data?

```
10      READ X, Y, Z
11      PRINT X, Y
12      PRINT Z
13      GO TO 10

900     DATA 3, 5.2, 8, 9
901     DATA 7, 10, 12
902     DATA 13, 15
```

5. What output would be produced by the following program?

```
50    LET I = 1
51    PRINT I,
52    IF I > 12 THEN 55
53    LET I = I + 1
54    GO TO 51
55    PRINT "    END"
56    STOP
```

Answers

1. (a) Labels may not include quotation marks. The reason is obvious;
        the computer would regard this as two labels—"NUMBER EARN-
        ING" and "REGULARLY"—with the word BREAD trapped be-
        tween them.
    (b) The statement is legal. The value of A + B will be printed in the
        first zone; the value of C will be printed in the second zone, and
        the label,

$$X = , X$$

will be printed in the third zone. Perhaps this is what the programmer intended. More likely he meant:

$$PRINT \ A + B, \ C, \ "X = ", \ X$$

    (c) This is perfectly legal since 3, 5.8, and 9 are all valid expressions
        (their values are, of course, 3, 5.8, and 9 respectively).
    (d) This is thoroughly illegal. You can read a number into box A and
        a second one into box B. But you cannot read a number into box
        C + D, because there is no such box. Numbers cannot be read
        into expressions; they can only be read into variables (boxes).
    (e) This is illegal. Commas are used to *separate* variable names in
        READ statements. The dangling comma is used *only* in PRINT
        statements.

2. This is an easy one. Just print nothing (one or more blanks) in the first
    zone, then tab:

$$PRINT \ " \ ", \ "HELLO"$$

3. Even easier. Just print seven blanks followed by X:

$$PRINT \ " \qquad X"$$

4.

3	5.2
8	
9	7
10	
12	13
15	

5.

1	2	3	4	5
6	7	8	9	10
11	12	13	END	

Chapter Five

Loops

One of the most useful techniques in programming involves the *loop*—the repeated execution of a series of statements with one or more changes made each time. Several loops have already been written; most programs contain so many that it is desirable to be able to write them succinctly. This chapter describes the FOR and NEXT commands. They allow you to replace several statements with two and, equally important, to make the structure of a loop much more obvious to anyone reading your program (including you).

FOR and NEXT

It is obviously senseless to repeat a series of statements unless something changes each time. Usually (but not always) the thing that changes is the value of some variable. In the typical case the variable is set at some *initial value* and the relevant statements executed. Then the variable is changed (*stepped*) by some amount (up or down) and the statements executed again. Eventually the variable will pass some desired *terminal value;* at this point the computer is expected to proceed with the remainder of the program.

Assume that you want to compute and print the present value of a dollar at an interest rate of 5 percent under various assumptions concerning

39

the year in which the dollar becomes available. If it turns up in year N, the present value is

$$P = 1/(1.05 \uparrow N)$$

The following loop would compute and print the desired values for years 1 through 25:

```
10    LET N = 1

20    LET P = 1 / (1.05↑N )
21    PRINT "   YEAR   ", N
22    PRINT "PRESENT VALUE =",  P
23    PRINT

30    IF N >= 25 THEN 40
31    LET N = N + 1
32    GO TO 20

40    STOP
```

In this case the variable that changes as the loop is executed over and over is N; its initial value is 1, its terminal value is 25, and the step is 1. Statements 10, 30, 31, and 32 take care of the housekeeping required to perform the operations in the desired manner. The loop itself consists of statements 20 through 23. When the looping is finished the computer is supposed to go to statement 40 (which is the end of the program in this case).

A simpler way to write the program is as follows:

```
10    FOR N = 1 TO 25 STEP 1
20        LET P = 1 / (1.05↑N )
21        PRINT "   YEAR   ", N
22        PRINT "PRESENT VALUE =",  P
23        PRINT
30    NEXT N

40    STOP
```

Not only are there fewer statements (two statements have replaced four), but the key information is contained in one statement (number 10), where it is more obvious to the reader (and to the programmer).

The statements comprising a loop written in this manner fall between the FOR statement and its associated NEXT statement. The variable to be altered when the loop is repeated is indicated in both statements; immediately after the command FOR and again after NEXT. The initial, terminal, and step values are indicated in that order in the FOR statement. The general form is this:

FOR *variable = initial value* TO *terminal value* STEP *step value*

Any or all of the three values may be indicated by expressions:

FOR X = A + B TO 3 * X STEP N

The STEP may be omitted; it will then be assumed to be one:

FOR Z = 1 TO 25

What does the computer do when it encounters a FOR statement? First, it sets the variable to the indicated initial value. Then it tests to see if it is already past the indicated terminal value; if so, it immediately transfers to the statement following the associated NEXT command. If not, the statements in the loop are executed. When the NEXT command is encountered, the computer adds (algebraically) the step value to the current value of the variable and tests again to see if it has passed the terminal value. If so, it goes on to the statements following the NEXT statement. If not, it goes back to the statement following the FOR statement. The process continues as long as necessary.

We have said (rather vaguely) that looping is terminated when the variable "passes" the specified terminal value. Just what does this mean? The answer is that it depends on the step being used. If the step size is positive, it means that the variable *exceeds* the terminal value (since the loop involves increasing values of the variable). If the step size is negative, it means that the variable is *smaller* (algebraically) than the terminal value (since the loop involves decreasing values of the variable). Needless to say, the step size should never be zero; this would imply that you wanted the computer to loop forever.

It is a good idea to avoid altering any variables mentioned in the FOR statement while you are in the loop. You may, if you wish, transfer out of a loop (with an IF or GO TO command). But you should avoid any subsequent transfer back into the middle of the loop unless no variables in the FOR statement have been changed in the meantime.

Loops may be nested inside each other. For example,

$$\text{FOR } I = 1 \text{ TO } 10$$
$$\text{FOR } J = 1 \text{ TO } 10$$
$$\cdot$$
$$\cdot$$
$$\cdot$$
$$\text{NEXT } J$$
$$\text{NEXT } I$$

They may *not* "cross" as in the following example:

$$\text{FOR } I = 1 \text{ TO } 10$$
$$\text{FOR } J = 1 \text{ TO } 10$$
$$\text{NEXT } I$$
$$\text{NEXT } J$$

All this may sound as if FOR-NEXT statements are more bother than they are worth. But in most cases you will find that they work quite nicely if you simply do what seems natural. The details indicated above to avoid possible problems are relevant only for cases in which a programmer attempts something exotic.

Examples

A few examples may be helpful. First, assume that you want to produce a table showing the present value of a dollar at 1, 2, 3, and 4 percent when the dollar becomes available in years 1 through 25. One way of doing this is as follows:

```
10    REMARK -- HEAD TABLE
12    PRINT "          PRESENT VALUE OF A DOLLAR"
13    PRINT
14    PRINT "YEAR","1 PCNT","2 PCNT","3 PCNT","4 PCNT"
15    PRINT

19    REMARK -- COMPUTE AND PRINT VALUES
20    FOR N = 1 TO 25
21        LET P1 = 1 / (1.01↑N)
22        LET P2 = 1 / (1.02↑N)
23        LET P3 = 1 / (1.03↑N)
24        LET P4 = 1 / (1.04↑N)
25        PRINT N, P1, P2, P3, P4
26        PRINT
27    NEXT N

30    STOP
```

A somewhat more compact way of writing it is the following:

```
10      REMARK -- HEAD TABLE
12      PRINT "          PRESENT VALUE OF A DOLLAR"
13      PRINT
14      PRINT "YEAR","1 PCNT","2 PCNT","3 PCNT","4 PCNT"
15      PRINT

19      REMARK -- COMPUTE AND PRINT VALUES
20      FOR N = 1 TO 25
21          PRINT N,
22          FOR R = .01 TO .04 STEP .01
23              PRINT 1/((1+R)↑N) ,
24          NEXT R
25          PRINT
26      NEXT N

30      STOP
```

In this simple approach, the inner loop spins R from .01 through .04 for each value of N from 1 to 25. Never again need you stand in awe of those massive tables of interest calculations found in so many reference books.

The next example illustrates the use of a loop to decrease the value of a variable. Assume that you want to read a number (call it N) and compute its factorial (F). The factorial of a number is found by multiplying it by itself less one, then by itself less two, and the like, until you get to one. In other words,

$$F = N * (N - 1) * (N - 2) * \ldots * 1$$

Now study the following program:

```
10      REMARK -- READ NUMBER, COMPUTE AND PRINT FACTORIAL
11      READ N
12      LET F = N
13      FOR M = N-1 TO 1 STEP -1
14          LET F = F * M
15      NEXT M
16      PRINT "FACTORIAL OF", N, "  = ", F
17      GO TO 11
```

See how it works? If not, play computer and follow the instructions with a number or two.

The final example is rather trivial. Assume that you want to skip five lines on the output sheet:

FOR K = 1 TO 5

PRINT

NEXT K

Admittedly, the variable (K) is not used at all inside the loop. But who said that it had to be?

FOR-NEXT loops are extremely helpful when dealing with lists and tables. But that discussion must be deferred until the next chapter.

Problems

1. Find any logical errors in the following program segment (part of a program):

```
10    FOR Z = 1 TO 30
11       IF Z = 5 THEN 10
12         PRINT Z
13    NEXT Z
```

2. Find any logical errors in the following program segment:

```
10    FOR Z = 1 TO 25 STEP -1
11       PRINT Z
12    NEXT Z
```

3. Write a program to read 18 pairs of numbers and to print the sum of each pair whenever the sum is less than 100.

4. Write a program to compute the factorials of the numbers 1 through 10.

5. Write a program using the FOR and NEXT commands rather extensively. Keep at it until you are convinced that you understand how to use them.

6. Most computers do their calculations with binary numbers (i.e., numbers to the base two, involving only zeros and ones). This can some-

times cause a problem when summing fractions. What kind of problem might arise, and how can it be solved?

Answers

1. The first time through the loop, Z will equal 1; the condition in statement 11 will not be met and Z will be printed. So far so good. The second time through, Z will be 2. Again, no problem. The difficulty will arise during the fifth time through: Z will equal 5 and the condition in statement 11 *will* be met. The computer will then transfer back to the FOR statement and start all over again. This portion of the program will thus try to produce an infinite set of output consisting of the numbers 1, 2, 3, 4, 1, 2, 3, 4, 1, 2, ... Presumably the programmer meant to have the computer avoid printing Z when it is 5. If so, he should have told it to go to the NEXT statement:

$$11 \quad \text{IF } Z = 5 \text{ THEN } 13$$

2. The step size here is negative. That means that the loop will be terminated as soon as the variable falls *below* 25. But its initial value (1) is already below 25. Thus the statement inside the loop (number 11) will never be executed.

3. Here is a possibility:

```
10    FOR I = 1 TO 18
11        READ X, Y
12        LET S = X + Y
13        IF S >= 100 THEN 15
14        PRINT S
15    NEXT I

16    STOP
```

Note that the variable (I) is not used inside the loop; the FOR-NEXT statements are simply there to count the times the loop has been executed.

4. Simply modify the example shown earlier:

```
10    FOR N = 1 TO 10
12        LET F = N
13        FOR M = N-1 TO 1 STEP -1
14            LET F = F * M
15        NEXT M
16        PRINT "FACTORIAL OF", N, "    = ", F
17    NEXT N

20    STOP
```

Note that this program requires no data (no problem: just give it none).

5. Never minimize the importance of writing actual programs and getting them to work correctly. It is the best way to learn programming.

6. Such complications rarely occur, but they can be irritating. The problem is the computer's inability to represent certain fractions with perfect accuracy as binary numbers (including some that can be easily represented as decimal fractions). Summing a number of such fractions may thus give a smaller total than expected. This should not be surprising, since it arises even with a desk calculator. For example,

$$1/3 + 1/3 + 1/3$$
$$= .33333333 + .33333333 + .33333333$$
$$= .99999999$$

which is slightly less than one.

The solution is simply to anticipate the possibility. For example, instead of saying:

$$\text{IF } T = 1 \text{ THEN } 100$$

say:

$$\text{IF } T >= .999999 \text{ THEN } 100$$

Note, however, that this kind of problem can occur only with fractions (and only with certain fractions at that). By and large, you need not worry about it.

Chapter Six

Lists and Tables

By now you should realize that it is possible to store many different numbers simultaneously. You just put them in different boxes (i.e., give them different variable names). Numbers can be put into a box with a READ statement or a LET statement. And once a number is in a box it can be referenced in any expression (e.g., in a LET, PRINT, or IF statement). But there is one problem that has undoubtedly plagued you already: if a group of numbers is to be stored concurrently, each must have a different name (i.e., be in a different box). And the number of names is rather limited.

To overcome this difficulty, and to allow more powerful techniques to be employed, programmers make extensive use of *lists* and *tables*. The general notion is simple. Imagine that you want to read and store the prices of eleven different items. You could say:

READ P0, P1, P2, P3, P4, P5, P6, P7, P8, P9, R0

But it would be much simpler if you could use a single letter to represent the type of information (e.g., P for price) and then refer to the prices as P(1), P(2). . . . Continuing with the analogy of mailboxes, you would refer to a box by its street (P) and the number on the street. Thus P(3) would refer to box 3 on P street, and P(11) to box 11 on P street. More relevant for our purposes, P(3) would refer to the third item in *list* P,

P(11) to the eleventh item, and so forth. The use of such lists will greatly expand the range of problems that you can program easily. And the use of tables will expand it even further.

Lists

You may arbitrarily decide to use any letter for the name of a list. The particular item in the list is indicated within parentheses immediately following the name of the list. Thus:

> A(3) is the third item in list A
> Z(93) is the ninety-third item in list Z

Remember that only a single letter may be used for the name of a list (or table, for that matter). Thus A9(3), for example, is quite illegal. Remember also to be consistent: once you have appropriated a letter to serve as the name of a list or table you should not use it for anything else.

How many items may there be in each list? Unless you tell it otherwise, the computer will make provisions for a limited number.[1] How does it know that you have decided to use a particular letter for the name of a list? It looks over your program before going to work; if it sees a letter followed by a parentheses it figures out what you are up to and acts accordingly.

You may refer to the number in a particular box in a list by giving the item number explicitly:

> A(3)
> A(92)

or implicitly, using any legal expression:

> A(Z)
> B(Q3)
> C(A + (B * D))

When the item number is indicated implicitly, the computer:

1. Evaluates the expression inside the parentheses
2. Rounds the result to the nearest integer (whole number), and then
3. Uses the appropriate item in the list

It is imperative that you understand this procedure perfectly. For example, there is no such thing as A(I) or A(J); there is an item in box A(1), another in box A(2), and so on. Whenever the computer encounters A(I)

---

1. Dartmouth/GE systems provide for items 0 through 10; UWBIC provides for items 0 through 120.

during the execution of the program it looks at the current value of I, substitutes it, and then finds the desired item in list A. The following example illustrates the procedure.

Assume that at the moment,

$$I = 3$$
$$J = 3$$
$$K = 6$$

Then,

A(I) refers to A(3)—   the third item in list A
A(J) refers to A(3)—   the third item in list A
A(K) refers to A(6)—   the sixth item in list A
A(I + J) refers to A(6)—the sixth item in list A

You may refer (explicitly or implicitly) to any item number in the list in question for which space has been reserved (of course you need not use all the reserved spaces). If you ever attempt to refer to an item for which space has not been reserved (e.g., a negative item number or one exceeding the space reserved) the computer will complain.

The idea of a list is very similar to the notion of a subscripted variable used in mathematics. Thus the mathematician might write X_3 to indicate the value of the third of a series of variables named X. We would write this as X(3). For this reason we often call lists (and tables, too, for that matter) *subscripted variables*. Regular variables are thus *unsubscripted variables*, and they are quite different. Note, for example, the difference between the unsubscripted variable P3 (the mailbox named P3) and the subscripted variable P(3)—the third item in list P.

One small point should be made here (although it may best be forgotten). For the convenience of mathematicians, the computer does reserve a box for the zero-th item on a list.

Reading Data into a List

Assume that you want to read twenty-five numbers into a list named X. Now the FOR statement really comes into its own:

```
10    FOR I = 1 TO 25
11        READ X(I)
12    NEXT I
```

The first time through the loop, I equals 1. When statement 11 is executed the computer reads a number from the data stack into box X(1)—the first box in list X. The second time through, I equals 2; the next number is thus read into X(2)—the second box in the list. And so it goes, until all twenty-five numbers have been placed in their appropriate boxes.

Perhaps you want to read thirty pairs of numbers into lists X and Y: the first pair into X(1) and Y(1), the second pair into X(2) and (Y2), and so forth. This presents no problem:

```
10    FOR I = 1 TO 30
11        READ X(I), Y(I)
12    NEXT I
```

As a final example, assume that the first number in the data stack tells how many pairs are to be read. Then you simply write the following:

```
 9    READ N
10    FOR I = 1 TO N
11        READ X(I), Y(I)
12    NEXT I
```

Sorting Data

An important operation with lists involves sorting data into either increasing or decreasing order. There are many ways of doing this; we will use one of the least efficient (but most easily understood).

Assume there are thirty numbers in list X and you want to rearrange them so they will be in order, with the largest number first and the smallest last. The trick is to compare pairs of adjacent numbers. If the first one is larger than the second (or equal to it), the pair is acceptable. If not, the numbers should be switched. Obviously if all pairs are acceptable the list is in the desired order. If not, it may or may not be. We thus want to pass through the list comparing all the adjacent pairs of numbers and recording the number of switches made. After completing a pass through the list, we check the number of switches. If none was made, the sorting is complete. If some pairs had to be switched, however, we pass through the list again to see if more switches are required. An example follows:

```
10    LET S = 0
11    FOR I = 1 TO 29
12        IF X(I) >= X(I+1) THEN 17
13        LET S = S + 1
14        LET Z = X(I)
15        LET X(I) = X(I+1)
16        LET X(I+1) = Z
17    NEXT I
18    IF S > 0 THEN 10
19    REMARK -- PROCEED
```

Note the way in which the switch is made. The number currently in box X(I) is stored temporarily in box Z. Then the number currently in box X(I + 1) is placed in box X(I). Finally, the number in box Z is placed in box X(I + 1). To see why all this is necessary, assume that

$$I = 8$$
$$X(8) = 12$$
$$X(9) = 15$$

Now follow these instructions:

$$\text{LET } X(I) = X(I + 1)$$
$$\text{LET } X(I + 1) = X(I)$$

Obviously this would have disastrous results.

Note also that the FOR statement instructs the computer to let $I = 1$, $2, \ldots , 29$. Why not let I equal 30? Because this would cause a comparison between $X(30)$ and $X(31)$; and we want to sort only the first 30 numbers in list X.

What would happen if the comparison had been writen as

$$12 \quad \text{IF } X(I) > X(I + 1) \text{ THEN } 17$$

Nothing, fortunately, if no two numbers were equal. But had there been at least one pair of numbers with the same value, the process would have continued indefinitely (until the computer became disgusted and refused to have anything more to do with your program).

Finally, consider a problem in which you want to sort the values in increasing order. Just change the comparison to

$$12 \quad \text{IF } X(I) < = X(I + 1) \text{ THEN } 17$$

Enough about sorting. It must be done with care, but it can be very useful.

Printing Numbers from a List

Assume that you would like to print the first *N* numbers from list X in a single column (i.e., one number per line). Just write the following:

```
10   FOR I = 1 TO N
11      PRINT X(I)
12   NEXT I
```

If you would prefer to have the numbers printed in all five zones (i.e., from left to right on line 1, then on line 2, and so on), just add a comma:

```
10   FOR I = 1 TO N
11      PRINT X(I),
12   NEXT I
```

Recall that the dangling comma tells the computer that the next print command executed should begin in the next available zone. This holds even when the next print command executed is the same one (being executed again during a subsequent pass through the loop). After the looping is completed, however, it is a good idea to "clear" the system; otherwise the next print command (located somewhere else in the program) may begin its output in the middle of the page (i.e., in the next available zone). The simplest way to accomplish this is to give the command PRINT after printing the numbers from the list:

```
10   FOR I = 1 TO N
11      PRINT X(I),
12   NEXT I
13   PRINT
```

Of course there are many ways to print data contained in lists. Here is one last example:

```
20    PRINT "    I   ", "    X   ", "    Y   ", "    Z   "
21    FOR I = 1 TO M
22        PRINT I, X(I), Y(I), Z(I)
23    NEXT I
```

Finding the Largest Number in a List

We can illustrate the points made thus far with a simple program designed to read a set of prices and to find the largest one. We assume that the first data number indicates the number of prices and that each price is followed by an identifying item number. The program is designed to find the largest price, then print it and the item numbers of all items with that price (there may be more than one).

The technique is relatively straightforward. Initially, the price of the first item is taken as the (temporary) maximum. Each price is then compared with the (current) maximum. If the new price is equal or smaller, no change is made. But if the new price is greater, it becomes the new (temporary) maximum. When all prices have been processed, the temporary maximum is clearly the real maximum. A second pass through the data is use to find the item numbers with that price. The program follows:

```
10    READ N

20    FOR K = 1 TO N
21        READ P(K), I(K)
22    NEXT K

30    LET M = P(1)
31    FOR K = 2 TO N
32        IF P(K) <= M THEN 34
33        LET M = P(K)
34    NEXT K

40    PRINT "MAXIMUM PRICE IS ", M
41    PRINT "ITEM NUMBERS FOLLOW "

50    FOR K = 1 TO N
51        IF P(K) <> M THEN 53
52        PRINT I(K),
53    NEXT K
54    PRINT

60    STOP
```

Obviously the *smallest* price (and associated item numbers) could have been found if the comparison had been written as:

$$32 \quad \text{IF } P(K) > = M \text{ THEN } 34$$

Tables

Lists are very useful, but for some problems they are not enough. For example, you might be interested in ten cities. You could easily use lists to refer to the altitudes of the cities (e.g., A(1), A(2), and the like) or to their populations (e.g., P(1), P(2), and the like), but you might also want to refer to the distances between pairs of cities. For this you would need a *table*—one probably named D. The number in the third row and fifth column (showing the distance between city 3 and city 5) could be described most simply as

$$D(3, 5)$$

And that is exactly how it would be described. You may appropriate any (single) letter to represent the name of a table. The particular item in the table is indicated in parentheses, with the row number first and the column number second. The row and column numbers must be separated by a comma. Either or both may be indicated implicitly, using any legal expression:

$$D(3, 5)$$
$$D(I, 5)$$
$$D(I, J)$$
$$D(A + B, \ 8)$$
$$D(3, \ X/Y)$$
$$D(A + B, \ X(I))$$

When an implicit row or column number is given, the computer evaluates the expression and then rounds the result to the nearest integer to determine the relevant row and/or column in the table. Both row and column number are checked to insure that space has been reserved for the item in question. If you do not explicitly reserve space, the computer will provide enough for you to use row numbers as great as 10 and column numbers as great as 10. Although you need not use them, row zero and column zero are also provided.

How does the computer know that you have decided to use a letter for a table? By looking over your program. If it finds a letter followed by a set of parentheses with a comma inside, it isn't very difficult to guess what you have in mind. But be consistent—if you decide to use a letter for a table name, do not use it for the name of a list (and vice versa).

As an example, assume that you want to set up a table of distances for ten cities. Each set of three data numbers describes a direct route between two cities. For example,

$$901 \quad DATA \ 3, \ 5, \ 275$$

indicates that there is a route connecting cities 3 and 5 and that the distance is 275 miles. In the table, the number 275 should thus be entered in row 3, column 5 and row 5, column 3.

What about the distance from a city to itself? It obviously is zero. Thus $D(1, 1)$ should be set to zero, as should $D(2, 2)$, $D(3, 3)$, and so on. What about cities not connected directly? We want the table to show a very long distance (9999 miles, to be specific) for such cases.

The instructions required to set up the table are relatively simple. First all entries are set to 9999, except those along the diagonal ($D(1,1)$, $D(2,2)$, and so forth), which are set to zero. Then sets of data are read and the distances entered in the appropriate positions in the table (throwing out the previously entered values of 9999). The final set of data is assumed to consist of negative numbers, signaling the end of this phase of the problem.

The program segment follows:

```
10      REMARK -- SET UP 9999 VALUES AND ZEROES ON DIAGONAL
20      FOR I = 1 TO 10
30        FOR J = 1 TO 10
31          IF I = J THEN 35
32          REMARK -- THIS IS NOT ALONG THE DIAGONAL
33          LET D(I,J) = 9999
34          GO TO 37
35          REMARK -- THIS IS ALONG THE DIAGONAL
36          LET D(I,J) = 0
37        NEXT J
38      NEXT I

40      REMARK -- READ A SET OF DATA
41        READ C1, C2, M
42      REMARK -- TEST FOR A NEGATIVE NUMBER
43        IF C1 < 0 THEN 50
44      REMARK -- ENTER DISTANCE
45        LET D(C1,C2) = M
46        LET D(C2,C1) = M
47      REMARK -- GO BACK TO READ ANOTHER SET OF DATA
48        GO TO 40

50      REMARK -- PROCEED
```

If you find this difficult to understand, remember the advice given earlier: play computer. If a machine can understand these instructions, why not you?

Reserving Space

We have said that the computer will automatically reserve space for lists and tables. But you may want it to provide more or less space than it would normally give you (more when you need more; less when you need less and the space is required for other lists and/or tables). To do this you indicate the desired dimensions *explicitly* in a DIM (for dimension) statement:

$$10 \quad \text{DIM A(250)}$$
$$500 \quad \text{DIM B(3)}$$
$$3150 \quad \text{DIM X(8, 15)}$$

The first statement reserves space for 250 items in list A (plus A(0)). The second statement reserves space for three items in list B (plus B(0)). The third statement reserves space for eight rows and fifteen columns in table X (plus row 0 and column 0). You may reserve space for more than one list and/or table with a single DIM statement; the entries are simply separated by commas:

$$5 \quad \text{DIM A(250), B(3), X(8, 15)}$$

DIM statements may appear anywhere in a program—the computer will find them before it goes to work. Remember, the space to be reserved must be indicated *explicitly*—no expressions allowed.

A Small Restriction

Generally you may use a subscripted variable (list or table reference) anywhere you are allowed to use a simple (unsubscripted) variable. There is one exception, however. The variable altered during execution of a FOR-NEXT loop must be an unsubscripted variable. This limitation refers *only* to the variable mentioned immediately after FOR in the FOR statement (and again after NEXT in the NEXT statement). The initial, terminal, and step values may involve any expression at all, including subscripted variables.

Problems

1. Table Z has ten rows and ten columns. Write a set of statements to set all the entries to zero.

2. What output will be produced by the following program?

```
10    FOR I = 1 TO 8
11        LET B(I) = 2 * I
12    NEXT I

20    FOR J = 1 TO 6
21        PRINT B(J),
22    NEXT J

30    STOP
```

3. What output will be produced by the following program?

```
10    FOR K = 1 TO 4
11        LET Q(K,K) = 9
12    NEXT K

20    FOR K = 1 TO 4
21        FOR L = K+1 TO 4
22            LET Q(K,L) = 1
23        NEXT L
24    NEXT K

30    FOR K = 1 TO 4
31        FOR L = 1 TO K-1
32            LET Q(K,L) = 0
33        NEXT L
34    NEXT K

40    FOR K = 1 TO 4
41        FOR L = 1 TO 4
42            PRINT Q(K,L),
43        NEXT L
44        PRINT
45    NEXT K

50    STOP
```

4. Assume that you have been asked to expand the program given in this chapter for setting up the table of distances for direct routes between pairs of cities. Add the necessary instructions to find and print the shortest distance from city 1 to each of the other cities. Hints:

   (a) Let $S(J)$ be the shortest distance from city 1 to city J.
   (b) To get started, let $S(J) = D(1, J)$.

(c) Now, assume that S(3) is the current shortest distance from city 1 to city 3, and that S(3) + D(3, 5) is less than the current value of S(5); what would you do?

(d) In general, assume that S(I) + D(I, J) is less than S(J); what would you do?

Remark: This is a difficult problem. If you conquer it, you are well on your way to programming rather complicated procedures; however, even if you fail, the situation is far from hopeless.

Answers

1.

```
10      FOR I = 1 TO 10
11         FOR J = 1 TO 10
12            LET Z(I,J) = 0
13         NEXT J
14      NEXT I
```

If row zero and column zero are to be cleared, statements 10 and 11 should, of course, run from 0 to 10 (e.g., FOR I = 0 TO 10). It is good practice to "clear" lists and tables in this manner before starting processing. In some cases it is absolutely essential.

2.

2	4	6	8	10
12				

Remember that there is no B(I) or B(J); just B(1), B(2), and so on.

3.

9	1	1	1
0	9	1	1
0	0	9	1
0	0	0	9

If you didn't get this right, get out a piece of paper and play computer, doing exactly what the instructions tell you to do.

4. The program statements through and including line 50 are the same as those shown in the earlier example. A possible set of additional statements to solve the problem follows:

```
51      REMARK -- SET UP INITIAL VALUES
52      FOR J = 2 TO 10
53         LET S(J) = D(1,J)
54      NEXT J

60      REMARK -- CHECK EACH VALUE FOR POSSIBLE IMPROVEMENT
61      LET Z = 0
62      FOR J = 2 TO 10
63         FOR I = 2 TO 10
64            IF I = J THEN 69
65            IF (S(I)+D(I,J)) >= S(J) THEN 69
66            REMARK -- SHORTER ROUTE FOUND
67            LET Z = 1
68            LET S(J) = S(I) + D(I,J)
69         NEXT I
70      NEXT J
71      IF Z = 1 THEN 60

80      REMARK -- PRINT RESULTS
82      FOR J = 2 TO 10
83         IF S(J) = 9999 THEN 86
84         PRINT "SHORTEST DISTANCE TO",J,"FROM 1 =", S(J)
84         GO TO 87
86         PRINT "CITY", J, "CANNOT BE REACHED FROM CITY 1"
87      NEXT J

90      STOP
```

To see how the program works, use the following data:

```
901      DATA 1, 2, 10
902      DATA 1, 4, 50
903      DATA 2, 3, 90
904      DATA 2, 4, 30
905      DATA 3, 4, 40
906      DATA -1, -1, -1
```

Chapter Seven

Functions and Subroutines

We have discussed many of the features of BASIC. Only two remain to be described here: functions and subroutines.

Functions

Periodically you may want to calculate some type of *function*—for example, you may want to find the logarithm of a number. Several of the more useful functions of this type can be obtained by simply asking for them. The function desired is indicated by a three-letter name. The value to be used is indicated explicitly or implicitly in parentheses following the function name. Thus LOG(8) refers to the natural logarithm of eight, and LOG(A + B) to the natural logarithm of the number found by adding A to B. The expression in the parentheses is called the *argument* of the function; it is evaluated and the resulting number used as indicated.

A function may be used in any expression. For example:

$$10 \quad \text{LET} \ Z = A + \text{LOG}(3)$$
$$20 \quad \text{LET} \ Q3 = A + (5 * \text{LOG}(3))$$
$$30 \quad \text{IF} \ B + \text{LOG}(C) > 50 \ \text{THEN} \ 433$$
$$40 \quad \text{PRINT} \ \text{LOG}(C)/\text{LOG}(B + 8)$$

When the computer encounters a function, it

1. Evaluates the expression in the parentheses
2. Applies the rules specified for the function in question (e.g., takes the logarithm of the number), and then
3. Uses the resulting number as if it had appeared instead of the function name and its argument

Nine of the functions available for the asking are described below. For convenience each is written here with an argument of X, but of course the argument may be any legal expression.

Function	Gives
LOG(X)	The natural logarithm of X. If X is negative, the computer takes the logarithm of its absolute value.
EXP(X)	The value obtained by raising e to the x-th power.
ABS(X)	The absolute value of X.
SQR(X)	The square root of X. If X is negative, the computer takes the square root of its absolute value.
INT(X)	The integer part of X. For example: If X is 9.8, INT(X) = 9; If X is -9.8, INT(X) $= -9$.
SIN(X)	The sine of X; X must be expressed in radians.
COS(X)	The cosine of X; X must be expressed in radians.
TAN(X)	The tangent of X; X must be expressed in radians.
ATN(X)	The arctangent of X; the arctangent is given in radians.

Random Numbers

A computer may be used to simulate events that happen in a somewhat random manner. One way to do this would involve reading in as data a list of random numbers. However, this is not necessary, for the computer acts as if it has its own list already (actually it computes numbers as required, but you need not concern yourself with such details). Each number in the list lies between zero and one. If you were to produce a great many of them, you would find that they fall rather uniformly over the range (in other words, the numbers come from a uniformly distributed population of random numbers between zero and one). You can get the next number from the list by simply asking for it in the following manner:[1]

$$RND(1)$$

This can appear in any expression; in form it is like the regular functions, although its value is obtained in a very different manner. When the computer encounters RND(1), it simply substitutes the next number from its list of random numbers and proceeds.

For example, the following program:

1. Actually any argument may be given, because it is not used.

```
10    FOR I = 1 TO 5
11       LET Z = RND(1)
12       PRINT Z
13    NEXT I
14    STOP
```

might generate the following output:

$$
\begin{array}{l}
.151432 \\
.901628 \\
.012963 \\
.511318 \\
.770312
\end{array}
$$

To simulate the results obtained by flipping a coin five times, just write the following:

```
20    FOR I = 1 TO 5
21       IF RND(1) <= .5 THEN 24
22       PRINT "HEADS"
23       GO TO 25
24       PRINT "TAILS"
25    NEXT I
26    STOP
```

Each time statement 21 is executed, a random number (the next one in the list) will be obtained; if it is greater than .5, the computer will print HEADS; if it is not, the computer will print TAILS.

Would you like a random number between 0 and 38? Just write this:

$$10 \quad \text{LET } R = 38 * RND(1)$$

Obviously 38 times a number falling between 0 and 1 must give a number between 0 and 38. If you would like R to be an integer between 1 and 38, just write this:[2]

$$10 \quad \text{LET } R = INT (1 + (38 * RND(1)))$$

One problem may bother you. The first time RND(1) is encountered, the first number in the computer's random number list is substituted; the

---

2. In the unlikely event that the random number turns out to be exactly 1.0, this statement would set R to 39. To insure against this, you could follow line 10 with

$$11 \quad \text{IF } R = 39 \text{ THEN } 10$$

second time, the second number is substituted, and so forth. If you want to start at a different place in the list each time you run your program, merely tell the computer to look at some of the initial entries. Then it will begin the real work with numbers lying farther down in the list. For example, preface the actual computations with

```
10    READ N
11    FOR I = 1 TO N
12       LET X = RND(1)
13    NEXT I
```

Subroutines

By now you have undoubtedly had the following experience: you have a procedure requiring several statements; moreover, the procedure needs to be followed in several places in your program. It is obviously a bother to rewrite all the statements repeatedly in every part of the program in which the procedure must be followed. You need some way to write the statements once and then refer to them as required. To do this you write the procedure as a *subroutine*. Whenever you want to execute the latter, you tell the computer to go to the beginning of the subroutine, but to remember where it was before beginning the subroutine. When the statements in the latter have been executed, the computer is expected to return to the appropriate place in the program.

The two new statements required for subroutines are GOSUB and RETURN. GOSUB is similar to a GO TO; the difference is that when the computer is told to GO TO 200, it goes to line 200 and promptly forgets where it was when it transferred there. But when it is told to GOSUB 200, it transfers to line number 200 and remembers where it was prior to the transfer. Later, when the computer encounters a RETURN statement, it will automatically go to the statement following the GOSUB from which it transferred.

To illustrate the use of subroutines, assume that the following statements occur somewhere in a program:

```
200    LET F = N
201    FOR M = N-1 TO 1 STEP -1
202       LET F = F * M
203    NEXT M
204    RETURN
```

This is the routine to compute the factorial of a number. Now assume that you want the factorial of some number, for example, X3. You simply put its value in box N and call in the subroutine:

```
10    LET N = X3
11    GOSUB 200
12    PRINT F
```

When the computer reaches statement 11, it transfers to statement 200, making a note of the fact that it got there from statement 11. Statement 200 is then executed, and the factorial is computed by the statements following it. Eventually statement 204 is reached. The computer then returns to the statement following number 11—statement 12.

Perhaps you need to calculate the factorial of X8 at some later point in your program. Just say:

```
56    LET N = X8
57    GOSUB 200
58    PRINT F
```

This example illustrates another advantage of the subroutine. Once you have written a set of statements to compute a factorial and checked them out to insure that they work, you can regard them as a "little black box." Any time you need a factorial, just write GOSUB 200. This is extremely helpful when you are writing large programs. You simply break the program into modules that are logically distinct, programming each as a subroutine. In fact, it is not unusual to encounter programs that look like this:

```
10    REMARK -- READ DATA
11        GOSUB 100
12    REMARK -- PROCESS DATA
13        GOSUB 200
14    REMARK -- PRINT DATA
15        GOSUB 300
16    REMARK -- RETURN TO PROCESS ANOTHER SET OF DATA
17        GO TO 10
```

The statements required to perform the desired operations would then follow. Although the first statement in a subroutine can be of any type, it is good practice to let it be a remark indicating the purpose of the subroutine:

100   REMARK—SUBROUTINE TO READ DATA

There are many advantages to be gained if programs are written in this modular manner. It is even possible to have different people program different parts of a problem. If course there must be close coordination so that the same variable will not be used inadvertently for different purposes in different subroutines.

You may have GOSUB statements within subroutines. For example, consider the following (nonsense) program:

```
10      READ N
11      GOSUB 100
12      PRINT Q, R, Z
13      STOP

100     REMARK -- SUBROUTINE A
101     LET Q = 2*N
102     GOSUB 200
103     LET R = Q/Z
104     RETURN

200     REMARK -- SUBROUTINE B
201     LET Z = 8
202     FOR I = 1 TO N
203         LET Z = I*Z
204     NEXT I
205     RETURN
```

When statement 11 is reached, the computer transfers to statement 100. It soon reaches statement 102, which sends it to statement 200. Eventually a RETURN is encountered at statement 205, and the computer returns to the place from which it departed most recently (in this case, statement 103). Later, upon encountering another RETURN it goes to statement 12, as intended.

You may place subroutines anywhere in your program, but be certain that the computer can only get to them via a GOSUB statement (if the computer encounters a RETURN statement when it has not come from anywhere via a GOSUB, it cannot continue). And be certain that you return from a subroutine via a RETURN statement; do not use a GO TO command for this purpose.

Playing Roulette

Many of the points in this chapter are illustrated in the following program. We assume that a prospective gambler wishes to try certain strategies for playing roulette in a simulated casino. His betting strategy is called a martingale. He begins with a basic bet (B); whenever he wins he returns to his basic bet. Whenever he loses, however, his next bet is double the previous (lost) amount—unless his money is insufficient, in which case he bets everything he has. The player continues until he either exhausts his capital or reach some predetermined upper limit (U).

Our gambler is convinced that his martingale strategy is sound, but he is uncertain as to whether he ought to put his money on number one each time or on "red" (there are fifteen red numbers). If he chooses the former he wins thirty-five times his bet if successful. If he chooses the latter his successes will be more frequent, but he will only win an amount equal to his bet each time. The gambler wants to be able to indicate in his data which of the two playing strategies is to be simulated. He also wants to be able to indicate whether or not a complete record of results (spin by spin) should be printed.

The program is relatively straightforward. The roulette wheel is assumed to have thirty-eight numbers and to be fair. Notice the extensive use of subroutines. This makes it easy to make changes in the program; for example, to alter strategies, calculate the effects of unbalanced wheels, and the like. Note also the use of P and S9 as "switches" to select the appropriate subroutines to be employed. Such techniques are essential for the professional programmer, and they can be valuable for you as well. The program follows:

```
10      REMARK -- PROGRAM TO SIMULATE ROULETTE PLAY

11      REMARK -- READ DATA
12          GOSUB 100
13      REMARK -- PERFORM INITIAL PROCESSING
14          GOSUB 200
15      REMARK -- SPIN WHEEL
16          GOSUB 250
17      REMARK -- FIND RESULTS (DEPENDING ON STRATEGY)
18      IF S9 = 1 THEN 21
19          GOSUB 300
20              GO TO 22
21          GOSUB 350
22      REMARK -- PRINT RESULTS IF DESIRED
23      IF P = 0 THEN 25
24          GOSUB 400
25      REMARK -- TEST FOR COMPLETION AND SELECT NEXT BET
26          GOSUB 500
```

```
27      REMARK -- SPIN AGAIN
28         GO TO 15

100     REMARK -- SUBROUTINE TO READ DATA
101     READ C, B, U, N, P, S9
102     PRINT "TOTAL CAPITAL =", C
103     PRINT "BASIC BET =", B
104     PRINT "UPPER LIMIT =", U
105     PRINT "INITIAL SPINS =", N
106     IF P = 0 THEN 109
107        PRINT "COMPLETE RECORD REQUESTED"
108           GO TO 110
109        PRINT "ONLY FINAL RESULTS REQUESTED "
110     IF S9 = 1 THEN 113
111        PRINT "STRATEGY IS TO BET ON RED EACH TIME"
112           GO TO 114
113        PRINT "STRATEGY IS TO BET ON 1 EACH TIME"
114        PRINT
115     RETURN

200     REMARK -- SUBROUTINE TO PERFORM INITIAL PROCESSING
201     REMARK -- MAKE INITIAL SPINS
202     FOR I = 1 TO N
203        LET Z = RND(1)
204     NEXT I
205     REMARK -- SET UP INITIAL WAGER
206     LET W = B
207     REMARK -- SET NUMBER OF SPINS TO ZERO
208     LET S = 0
209     RETURN

250     REMARK -- SUBROUTINE TO SPIN WHEEL
251     LET R = INT( 1 + (38*RND(1)) )
252     IF R = 39 THEN 251
253     LET S = S + 1
254     RETURN

300     REMARK -- SUBROUTINE FOR STRATEGY 0
301     IF R <= 15 THEN 306
302     REMARK -- LOST
303        LET O9 = 0
304        LET C = C - W
305        RETURN
306     REMARK -- WON
307        LET O9 = 1
308        LET C = C + W
309        RETURN

350     REMARK -- SUBROUTINE FOR STRATEGY 1
351     IF R = 1 THEN 356
352     REMARK -- LOST
353        LET O9 = 0
354        LET C = C - W
```

```
355       RETURN
356    REMARK -- WON
357       LET O9 = 1
358       LET C = C + ( 35*W )
359       RETURN

400    REMARK -- SUBROUTINE TO PRINT RESULTS OF A SPIN
401    PRINT "SPIN NUMBER", S
402    PRINT "YOU BET", W
403    PRINT "WHEEL CAME UP", R
404    PRINT "YOU NOW HAVE", C
405    PRINT
406    RETURN

500    REMARK -- TEST FOR COMPLETION AND SELECT NEXT BET
501    IF C = 0 THEN 520
502    IF C >= U THEN 530
503    REMARK -- PLAY AGAIN
504    IF O9 = 0 THEN 510
505    REMARK -- PREVIOUS BET WON
506       LET W = 8
507       GO TO 515
510    REMARK -- PREVIOUS BET LOST, DOUBLE IT
511       LET W = 2 * W
515    REMARK -- CHECK CAPITAL
516    IF C > W THEN 519
517    REMARK -- LOWER WAGER
518       LET W = C
519    RETURN

520    REMARK -- WIPED OUT
521       PRINT "SORRY -- WIPED OUT AFTER", S, "SPINS"
522       STOP
530    REMARK -- MADE IT
531       PRINT "UPPER LIMIT REACHED AFTER", S, "SPINS"
532       PRINT "YOUR CAPITAL IS NOW", C
533       PRINT "CONGRATULATIONS"
534    STOP
```

Canned Programs

Many people who use computers do not attempt to master a programming language at all; instead they simply rely on professional programmers who have (hopefully) anticipated their needs when preparing programs. Certainly one need not program his own routine to do regression analysis, or linear programming, or any of a number of generally utilized techniques. It is far more efficient for a professional programmer to devote his time to preparing a general-purpose, well-written, and highly efficient program for such an application. Such "production," "canned," or "package" programs should meet the following criteria:

1. They should be extremely simple to use; this means that input can be prepared by simply following a few straightforward instructions.

2. They should be truly general-purpose: several variations of the technique should be available with only a few alterations in input data required to obtain a different variation (unfortunately this criterion is often in conflict with the first).

3. They should provide output describing the results explicitly and requiring little or no knowledge of the underlying (solution) technique on the part of the user.

4. They should anticipate virtually any type of error that the user might make when preparing his input data; moreover, such errors should be identified on the output when detected.

5. Finally, they should be efficient (require minimal computer time) and thoroughly checked (they should work).

Appendix C contains five such programs, all written in BASIC. Of course the language in which a program is written is of little concern to the user who wants to do exactly what the program is designed to do. But it is not unusual to find that a few changes in the program will be required if it is to serve the exact purpose the user had in mind. Under these conditions the language used is important, as is the program's documentation. Since no program can be truly general-purpose, some canned programs are written as subroutines (or sets of subroutines); the user is expected to incorporate them in a program written to serve his particular needs. One package of this type is also included in Appendix C.

Concluding Remarks

This book has covered the essential constructs of BASIC. You are now in a position to write programs that will solve almost any numeric problem (or, putting it another way, that will process numeric data in almost any way). Needless to say, knowledge of a language is a necessary but not sufficient condition for problem-solving; you must also be able to *design* procedures for accomplishing the tasks you have in mind. BASIC provides a simple and succinct language for describing such procedures (often called *algorithms*). It offers, of course, an additional advantage of tremendous value—it can be used with many computer systems.

BASIC is but one of a great number of high-level computer-programming languages; and the number is increasing rapidly. If you are a serious student of computer programming, you will want to learn about several other languages. But this process will be much simpler than it would have been had you not studied a language such as BASIC at the outset.

Perhaps you are a serious student, but not deeply interested in computer programming. If so, the material covered here should suffice. You should now be able to use a computer as a research and/or clerical assistant. More important, you should have a considerable understanding of computer programming; if you and a professional programmer must work together at some time in the future, the experience should prove reasonably pleasant for both of you.

Finally, and perhaps most important of all, you now know something about computers. You know that they are *not* giant electronic brains, but that they *can* be programmed to do rather clever things; and you have a fair notion of the manner in which this is done. This knowledge alone should prove well worth the time, effort, and money you have expended.

Problems

1. Write a statement to round variable Z to the nearest integer (whole number); assume that Z is positive.

2. Write a statement to round variable Z to the nearest tenth (i.e., one decimal place); assume that Z is positive.

3. Assume that variable G represents gross pay in dollars. Write a statement to round it to the nearest cent.

4. Write a subroutine that will round variable A to the nearest value with N places to the right of the decimal point.

5. Write some statements to set up a list Z containing the logarithms of the first N numbers in some other list X.

6. How would you modify the program shown on pages 67, 68, and 69 if strategy one involved splitting the bet between numbers one and two?

7. How would you modify the program shown on pages 67, 68, and 69 to have the computer stop if play continues for a thousand spins?

Answers

1.

```
10   LET  Z = INT(Z + .5)
```

2.

```
10   LET  Z = .1 * INT((10 * Z) + .5)
```

3.

$$10 \quad \text{LET} \ G = .01 * \text{INT}((100 * G) + .5)$$

4.

$$100 \quad \text{LET} \ P = 10 \uparrow N$$
$$101 \quad \text{LET} \ A = (1/P) * \text{INT}((P * A) + .5)$$
$$102 \quad \text{RETURN}$$

5.

```
100    FOR I = 1 TO N
101       LET Z(I) = LOG(X(I))
102    NEXT I
```

6. Alter the print statement:

113 PRINT "STRATEGY IS TO BET 1 AND 2 EACH TIME"

Alter the subroutine for strategy one:

$$351 \quad \text{IF} \ R < = 2 \ \text{THEN} \ 356$$

.

.

.

$$358 \quad \text{LET} \ C = C + (35 * (W/2))$$

7. The solution is to check S each time. This can be done in any of a number of places in the program. For example:

```
26    GOSUB 500
27    IF S > 1000 THEN 30
28    REMARK -- SPIN AGAIN
29       GO TO 15
30    REMARK -- TOO MANY SPINS
31       GOSUB 400
32       STOP
```

Notice that you need not write a special set of statements to indicate the player's situation at this point; just GOSUB 400. This output would be particularly helpful if the user had not requested output after each spin.

Appendixes

The Dartmouth/GE System

Introduction

As indicated in the Preface, BASIC was developed at Dartmouth College under the direction of Professor J. G. Kemeny. The original version was implemented on a system that included two General Electric computers— a GE 235 and a Datanet 30 (together sometimes called a GE 265 system). Similar systems have been installed in a number of locations by the General Electric Company for use by subscribers on a "dial-up" basis. Dartmouth College has converted its original system to one based on a GE 625 computer, and General Electric (and others) now offer similar systems for subscribers. Needless to say, there are some differences among systems. Strictly speaking, the description in this Appendix applies only to the original Dartmouth system. However, most of the features are found in the other systems as well.

The key advantage of the Dartmouth/GE system is its rapid response time. The system uses *time-sharing*—a number of users sit at remote teletypewriter consoles, sharing the time of the computer system. In practice, each user is given the illusion that he has a computer to himself, since the system can usually service the users in round-robin fashion rapidly enough to keep up with their demands for input and output (needless to say, computers handle information much faster than teletypewriters). Users requesting large amounts of computation between input/ output operations may have to wait, because their work will be performed in pieces; however, the impression will be simply that the computer is not unusually fast.

The Dartmouth/GE system is but one of many time-shared services. Several commercial service bureaus offer BASIC on a Scientific Data Systems computer (the SDS 940). A version for use on the Burroughs 5500 has also been developed. And many other languages are available on various computer systems operating in a time-shared mode. This brief description of the manner in which the Dartmouth/GE system is used with BASIC will, however, suggest the power and convenience of the general approach.

Using the System

To begin a "conversation" with the computer, dial the computer's number and establish a connection (if no lines are available, you will get a busy signal). This process makes it possible to dial computers of various types located virtually anywhere in the country (or abroad, for that matter).

Once the connection is established, type

HELLO

After typing any line (including this one), you must press the RETURN key; this signals the computer that the end of a line has been reached and some action on its part is required.

The computer responds next by typing

USER NUMBER—

Simply fill in your identifying number and hit RETURN; the line will then look like this:

USER NUMBER—S10000

Next the computer will ask you to specify the system to be used; if it is BASIC, the line should look like this after you type your response:

SYSTEM—BASIC

The computer then asks

NEW OR OLD—

If you wish to enter a new BASIC program, type NEW. If you wish a former program to be retrieved from the location in which the computer has saved it, type OLD.

Finally, the computer asks for the problem name. This will be used to identify a new program or to select the appropriate old program to be retrieved.

If a new program is being entered, simply write lines in any order desired. The system will keep them in numeric order. To change a line, retype it with the same line number. To delete a line, just type the line number (followed, of course, by a RETURN).

At any point you may ask the computer to list your program. To list the entire program, type

LIST

To list the portion beginning with a particular line number, say 360, type

LIST—360

To stop a listing, type

STOP

When you are ready to run your program, type

RUN

Any time you would like your program (and data, for that matter) saved, simply type

SAVE

The material can be retrieved later by typing OLD and giving the program name when asked (after HELLO).

Many other operations are available for editing information, storing and retrieving files, merging programs, and so forth. However, the essential instructions are those described above; information about additional features is best obtained from those running the system you plan to use.

The Language

The language used with the Dartmouth/GE system includes the BASIC constructs described in the text. However, there are some additional commands and some variations on the commands we have described. The key differences are listed here.

END

First, and most important of all, the last (highest-numbered) line must be END. For example:

9999   END

This must come after all program statements and all DATA statements. It may be used as a STOP command, if desired. But it must be present and it must be last.

INPUT

The system allows users to read data from a data stack filled with one or more DATA statements, as described in the text. But it also allows the programmer to instruct the computer to get data from the person sitting at the teletypewriter when the program is being run. The command is INPUT, and it is written just as a READ command is written. Upon encountering an INPUT command, the computer prints a question mark followed by a space. It then waits for the required number(s) to be typed, followed by a carriage return.

The INPUT command allows one to write programs that will "converse" with the user. For example, consider the following portion of a regression program:

```
100   PRINT "HOW MANY OBSERVATIONS DO YOU HAVE"
101   INPUT N
```

This would cause the following message to appear at the teletype console:

HOW MANY OBSERVATIONS DO YOU HAVE?

The user would then answer and hit RETURN. The line would appear as follows:

HOW MANY OBSERVATIONS DO YOU HAVE?   4

The next part of the program might be

```
102   PRINT
103   PRINT "PLEASE GIVE THE VARIABLES FOR EACH
      OBSERVATION"
104   FOR I = 1 TO N
105   PRINT "OBSERVATION", I,
106   INPUT X(I), Y(I)
107   NEXT I
```

With the user's responses, the sheet would appear as follows:

HOW MANY OBSERVATIONS DO YOU HAVE?   4
PLEASE GIVE THE VARIABLES FOR EACH OBSERVATION
OBSERVATION 1? 23, 45.6
OBSERVATION 2? 15, −35.7

OBSERVATION 3? 17.5, 19.1
OBSERVATION 4? 21.2, 13

The INPUT command makes it possible to write programs which lead the user through the steps required to obtain information about his problem and then solve it. The person interested only in regression need know only how to say HELLO, to indicate that the system to be used is BASIC, that he wants an OLD program, and that its name is, e.g., REG***. From that point on, he simply follows the instructions given him by the computer.

Printing

As indicated in the text, the output sheet is divided into five zones of fifteen characters each, and a comma signals a "tab" to the beginning of the next zone. An alternative is to use a semicolon (;). This indicates that the teletype is to move to the beginning of the next multiple of three columns. Judicious use of the semicolon makes it possible to pack more information on a line. It also makes it possible to line up decimal points for numbers printed on different lines. Since the Dartmouth/GE system (unlike the UWBIC system) prints numbers starting at the beginning of the zone (or subzone) selected, there is no guarantee that numbers will be automatically lined up vertically.

If a label is followed by an expression, with no comma separating the two, the value of the expression will be printed immediately after the label (and not in the next zone, as with UWBIC). This will also be the case if a semicolon is used to separate the two items.

Lists and Tables

Unless a DIM statement is used, the Dartmouth/GE system reserves space for subscripts 0 through 10 inclusive for either lists or tables.

Functions

The Dartmouth/GE system allows the user to define some of his own functions (in addition to those provided automatically, as described in the text). The command is DEF. The function name must begin with FN and contain three letters (thus there are only twenty-six possibilities). A simple (unsubscripted) variable must be given as an argument in the definition. Since it will be used every time the function is referenced, it is a good idea to use a variable that does not appear elsewhere in the program. The expression to the right of the equal sign in the definition may involve other variables than the one used as an argument and any of the regular (built-in) functions, but no other user-defined functions are allowed.

An example may help to clarify the use of such functions. Consider the following:

$$10 \quad \text{DEF FNC}(Z) = Z \uparrow 3$$

Now assume that you write this:

$$300 \quad \text{LET } Q = A/(B + \text{FNC}(10))$$

The value 10 will be assigned to Z; then it will be cubed, giving 1000. This result will be used in place of the reference FNC(10) in statement 300.

Constants

Constants may be written as digits with or without a decimal point and/or sign as long as no more than nine digits are used. In addition, a number may be followed by the letter E (read "times ten to the power") and an integer. For example:

3E1 means 3 times 10 to the first power = 30
.35E − 5 means .35 times 10 to the −5 power = .0000035

Limitations

The limitations imposed by a system depend on both the computer(s) being used and the manner in which the system's capabilities are shared among users. The following limitations applied to the early Dartmouth/GE systems:

Length of program:	About two feet of teletype paper
Constants:	No more than 75 different constants in program statements
Data:	No more than 300 data numbers in DATA statements
FOR statements:	No more than 26 in the program
GO TO and IF-THEN statements:	No more than 80 in all
Lists and Tables:	The total number of elements in all lists and tables combined cannot exceed 2000

Appendix B

The UWBIC System

Introduction

The UWBIC system was developed at the University of Washington. It was designed to make it possible to run BASIC programs on medium-to-large-scale computers in a batch (card) mode. The system is, in essence, a program that accepts BASIC programs and their associated data as input, producing diagnostic messages and/or answers as output. The original system was written in FORTRAN IV (a high-level professional programmer's language). Fortunately, most computer manufacturers provide a FORTRAN IV-to-machine language translator for each of their major computers. By running the system through such a translator, a machine-language version of UWBIC can be produced for the type of computer to be used. This version can then be used to run BASIC programs. For convenience, it is typically stored on either a magnetic disk or tape; the user then need only precede his BASIC program with a card or two containing the information required to cause the system to be copied into the computer's main memory.

The UWBIC system is in operation at a number of installations on several different types of computers. Needless to say, there are some differences in procedure, language capabilities, and so on. Strictly speaking, the information that follows applies only to the standard system used on

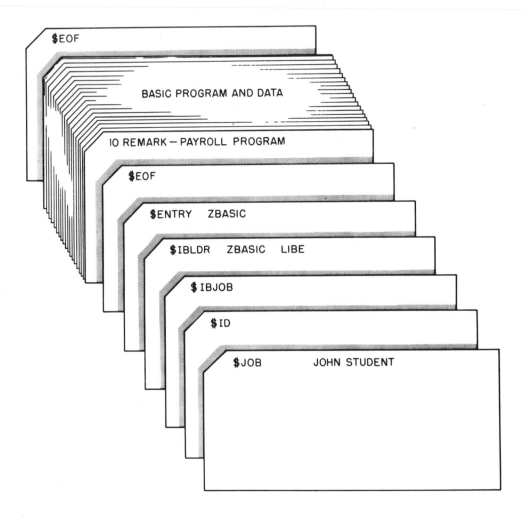

Figure B.1

an IBM 7094 (the machine on which it was first implemented). But any differences between it and other implementations will be relatively minor.

Using the System

UWBIC is a card-oriented system. Both program and data must be punched on 80-column cards, one per line. The cards must be submitted in order, with the first line at the front of the deck and the last at the end. Unlike the Dartmouth/GE system, only the order of the cards is relevant with UWBIC. Line numbers are thus optional, and need not be sequential. However, any given line number can be used only once.

Decks must typically begin and end with one or more control cards. For example, at the University of Washington, a typical deck for use with the IBM 7094 is depicted in Figure B.1.

Output, including a listing of the cards submitted (with or without diagnostic messages), is prepared on a high-speed printer. Since a number of jobs may be run together, this type of operation is often called the *batch* mode. Its disadvantage is obvious—the response (or *turnaround*) time can be very long. On the other hand, larger jobs can also be run, with substantial amounts of data.

The Language

As indicated in footnotes, the language used with the UWBIC system differs slightly from that described in the text. Moreover, a few additional features have been incorporated. The major changes are described below.

Character Set

Since standard keypunch machines lack some of the characters found on certain teletypewriters, UWBIC uses a character set that differs slightly from that described in the text. The changes required are

Instead of	*Use*
>	GT
>=	GE
<	LT
<=	LE
<>	NE
↑	**
"	'

END

The last card in a program must be an END. Like other cards, it may or may not have a line number. If desired, it may be used as a STOP command.

DATA

Data numbers may be included in DATA statements (with or without line numbers), as described in the text. All such statements must appear before END. However, data numbers (but *only* data numbers) may also appear after END. The data stack is filled with numbers as they are encountered in the deck. You may thus put numbers in DATA statements before END, on cards after END, or in both positions if you wish.

Data included after END may be preceded with the word DATA, although this is optional. Line numbers may *not* be used, however.

The amount of data that can appear in DATA statements before an END is limited (typically to one thousand numbers); the amount appearing after an END is, for all practical purposes, unlimited.

PAGE

UWBIC allows you to use the command PAGE. This instructs the computer to move the output sheet to the top of the next page (needless to say, this is done automatically whenever a page is filled).

PRINT ALL

A useful feature for checking a program is the command PRINT ALL. This causes the values of all variables greater than .00001 or less than —.00001 to be printed, one per line. For example:

$$A = 3.5$$
$$P = 4.9$$
$$Z9 = -1$$

The command should be used sparingly, since it can generate considerable output.

Printing

UWBIC attempts to print each number centered within its fifteen-column zone. If possible, the number is printed with the decimal point in the ninth column of the zone (if the number is an integer, however, the decimal point is not printed). In every case, six significant digits will be printed (except that trailing zeros to the right of the decimal point will be suppressed). If necessary, the decimal point will be moved as far as required to the right or left of the ninth column to print the number appropriately. If the number is either very small or very large, an exponential form will be printed (the letter E is read as "times ten to the power").

Lists and Tables

Unless mentioned in a DIM statement, subscripts for lists may range from 0 through 120 inclusive. The automatic dimensions for tables allow subscripts from 0 through 10 inclusive.

Miscellaneous

Blank cards may be included to improve the readability of the program listing. Several jobs may be run at once: simply separate each deck (program plus data) from the next with a card containing an asterisk in column one.

Limitations

The limitations imposed on UWBIC users depend largely on the computer system. As mentioned, data numbers in DATA statements are usually limited to one thousand, but any number may be included after END. There is an overall limit to program statements, lists and tables, constants, and such, but it is very difficult to state it simply; space not utilized for one purpose is made available for other purposes. In general it is possible to run very large programs and to accommodate lists and tables with several thousand elements.

Some Useful Programs

This Appendix contains several programs written in the BASIC language. They are included for one or more of the following reasons:

1. They may be useful in their own right.
2. They provide concrete examples of computer programs.
3. They illustrate the manner in which general-purpose programs are prepared.

Several criterial for general-purpose (canned) programs were given in Chapter 7. These programs do not meet all of the criteria. Indeed, production programs should typically be written in a language more efficient (in terms of computer time) than BASIC. Moreover, to illustrate the use of the language we have often utilized less efficient solution techniques than might be chosen for true production programs. However, these programs do work. And for small jobs they may prove adequate.

Each program is described briefly; the description is then followed by a summary of the form in which inputs are prepared, a brief discussion of the method used, the program itself, a set of test data, and the resulting output. The casual user need only read the first two sections, although he may want to glance at the last two sections also. The student of programming will want to read everything. The first five programs are complete and can be used by anyone. The last program illustrates the use of a set of subroutines; it is designed for those who have mastered the BASIC language.

No attempt is made to describe the technique used in each program. The user is presumed to know something about the type of problem the program is designed to solve. This suggests the desirability of studying the programs in conjunction with the study of the problems. Thus BCP might be studied in a production or industrial engineering class, BRC in a statistics class, BSAFM in a computer programming class, and so on.

The programs have been tested with the UWBIC system. However, for consistency, they are listed here in the format required for the Dartmouth/ GE system. As presently written, they may prove too large to run on some of the General Electric on-line systems.

The test data shown with each program have been prepared using DATA statements. Users of the UWBIC systems may prefer to place their data after the END card, omitting line numbers, remarks, and the word DATA.

Critical Path Problems (BCP)

Description

A *project* consists of *events* and *activities*. The events can be represented as points (nodes) and the activities as arrows (arcs) in a network. Each activity starts at one event (its predecessor) and ends at another (its successor). Moreover, each activity requires some amount of time to complete. Events are assigned numbers: the smallest to the event "begin project" and the largest to the event "end project." Events are numbered so that the predecessor for any activity has a lower number than the successor.

The key rule for completing a project is the following: no activity for which an event is a predecessor may start until *all* activities for which the event is the successor have been completed. Subject to this rule, the objective is to complete the project as soon as possible. Consistent with the estimate of the earliest project completion time are two times for each event. The first indicates the *earliest time* at which all activities for which the event is the successor can be completed. The second indicates the *latest time* at which all activities for which the event is the predecessor may be started without affecting the earliest possible project completion time (all other things being equal). If the earliest time equals the latest time the event is on the *critical path*. A similar analysis may be made for activities. The *maximum time* available to complete any given activity (all other things being equal) is obtained by starting the activity at the earliest time for its predecessor event and completing it at the latest time for its successor event. If this maximum time equals the (estimated) actual time, the *activity* is on the critical path.

BCP computes the earliest and latest times for each event and the maximum time for each activity. Events and activities on the critical path are also indicated. The earliest (and latest) time for the highest-numbered event represents the earliest time at which the entire project can be completed.

Inputs

Inputs for a project must be provided in the following order:

Number of first event
Number of second event

·

·

·

Number of last event

−1

No more than 200 events
Events need not be in order

Predecessor of first activity
Successor of first activity
Time for first activity

Predecessor of second activity
Successor of second activity
Time for second activity

·

·

·

Predecessor of last activity
Successor of last activity
Time for last activity

No more than 500 activities
Activities need not be in order

−1
−1
−1

Additional projects may be analyzed; the inputs described above are simply repeated.

Method

The program operates in two major phases. The first phase calculates the earliest time for each event. Activities are ranked in ascending order on the basis of predecessor event, and the earliest time for each event is set to zero. Each activity is then processed; if the sum of its time plus the earliest time of its predecessor exceeds the current earliest time of its successor, the latter is replaced with the sum. Because activities go from lower-numbered to higher-numbered events, and because activities are processed in order, one pass through the activities yields the final set of earliest event times. The earliest time for the highest-numbered event is, of course, the earliest time at which the entire project can be completed.

The second phase of the program calculates the latest time for each event. In essence the method merely repeats the procedure of phase one, going backwards through the network; the resulting times are then subtracted from the earliest project completion time. The program accomplishes this by re-ranking the activities in descending order of successor event and then following essentially the procedure of phase one. The results are then printed with "critical path" indicated where appropriate.

Each program begins on a separate page.

Program

```
 5   REMARK -- CRITICAL PATH PROGRAM

 7   DIM N(201), E(201), L(201), P(501), S(501), T(501), R(501)

10   REMARK -- N(I) IS THE NUMBER OF EVENT I
11   REMARK -- E(I) IS THE EARLIEST TIME FOR EVENT I
12   REMARK -- L(I) IS THE LATEST TIME FOR EVENT I
13   REMARK -- N1 IS THE NUMBER OF EVENTS
20   REMARK -- P(I) IS THE EVENT PRECEEDING ACTIVITY I
21   REMARK -- S(I) IS THE EVENT SUCCEEDING ACTIVITY I
22   REMARK -- T(I) IS THE TIME TO COMPLETE ACTIVITY I
23   REMARK -- R(I) IS THE NUMBER OF THE I"TH-RANKED ACTIVITY
24   REMARK -- N2 IS THE NUMBER OF ACTIVITIES
30   REMARK -- C IS THE MINIMUM TIME TO COMPLETE THE PROJECT

40   REMARK -- READ EVENTS
41   GOSUB 200

50   REMARK -- READ ACTIVITIES
51   GOSUB 300

60   REMARK -- RANK ACTIVITIES ON ASCENDING PREDECESSOR NUMBER
61   LET N5 = 0
62   GOSUB 400

70   REMARK -- FIND EARLY EVENT TIMES
71   GOSUB 500

80   REMARK -- FIND LATE EVENT TIMES
81   GOSUB 700

90   REMARK -- PRINT EVENT TIMES
91   GOSUB 800

95   REMARK -- PRINT ACTIVITY TIMES
96   GOSUB 900

98   REMARK -- RETURN TO READ A NEW PROBLEM
99   GO TO 40
```

```
200    REMARK -- SUBROUTINE TO READ EVENT NUMBERS
210    FOR I = 1 TO 201
211        LET E(I) = 0
212        LET L(I) = 0
213        READ N(I)
214        IF N(I) <= 0 THEN 230
215    NEXT I
220    PRINT "SORRY -- I CAN ONLY HANDLE 200 EVENTS"
221    STOP
230    LET N1 = I - 1
231    RETURN

300    REMARK -- SUBROUTINE TO READ ACTIVITIES
310    FOR I = 1 TO 501
311        READ P(I), S(I), T(I)
312        IF P(I) <= 0 THEN 320
313    NEXT I
314    PRINT "SORRY -- I CAN ONLY HANDLE 500 ACTIVITIES"
315    STOP
320    LET N2 = I - 1
321    RETURN


400    REMARK -- SUBROUTINE TO ASSIGN RANKS TO ACTIVITIES
401    REMARK -- IF N5 = 0, RANK ON ASCENDING ORDER OF PREDECESSOR
402    REMARK -- IF N5 = 1, RANK ON DESCENDING ORDER OF SUCCESSOR

410    FOR I = 1 TO N2
411        LET R(I) = I
412    NEXT I
415    LET N9 = N2

420    LET N9 = N9 - 1
421    LET N8 = 0
422    FOR I = 1 TO N9
423        IF N5 = 1 THEN 426
424        IF P(R(I)) <= P(R(I+1)) THEN 431
425        GO TO 427
426        IF S(R(I)) >= S(R(I+1)) THEN 431
427        LET R1 = R(I)
428        LET R(I) = R(I+1)
429        LET R(I+1) = R1
430        LET N8 = 1
431    NEXT I
432    IF N8 = 1 THEN 420
440    RETURN
```

```
500    REMARK -- SUBROUTINE TO FIND EARLY EVENT TIMES
510    FOR I = 1 TO N2
511        LET N3 = P(R(I))
512        GOSUB 600
513        LET I1 = K
514        LET N3 = S(R(I))
515        GOSUB 600
516        LET I2 = K
517        IF E(I2) >= E(I1) + T(R(I)) THEN 519
518        LET E(I2) = E(I1) + T(R(I))
519    NEXT I
520    RETURN

600    REMARK -- SUBROUTINE TO FIND INTERNAL NUMBER (K) OF EVENT N3
610    FOR K = 1 TO N1
611        IF N(K) = N3 THEN 620
612    NEXT K
613    PRINT "SORRY -- YOU DIDNT TELL ME ABOUT EVENT", N3
614    STOP
620    RETURN

700    REMARK -- SUBROUTINE TO FIND LATE EVENT TIMES

710    REMARK -- RANK ACTIVITIES IN DESCENDING ORDER OF SUCCESSORS
711    LET N5 = 1
712    GOSUB 400

720    FOR I = 1 TO N2
721        LET N3 = S(R(I))
722        GOSUB 600
723        LET I1 = K
724        LET N3 = P(R(I))
725        GOSUB 600
726        LET I2 = K
727        IF L(I2) >= L(I1) + T(R(I)) THEN 729
728        LET L(I2) = L(I1) + T(R(I))
729    NEXT I

730    LET N3 = S(R(1))
731    GOSUB 600
732    LET C = E(K)
733    FOR I = 1 TO N1
734        LET L(I) = C - L(I)
735    NEXT I
740    RETURN
```

```
800   REMARK -- SUBROUTINE TO PRINT EVENT TIMES
810   PRINT
811   PRINT " ", " EVENT TIMES"
812   PRINT
820   PRINT "   EVENT", "EARLIEST TIME", "LATEST TIME"
821   PRINT

830   FOR I = 1 TO N1
831       IF E(I) = L(I) THEN 834
832       PRINT N(I), E(I), L(I)
833       GO TO 835
834       PRINT N(I), E(I), L(I), "CRITICAL PATH"
835   NEXT I
840   RETURN

900   REMARK -- SUBROUTINE TO PRINT ACTIVITY TIMES
910   PRINT
911   PRINT " ", "    ACTIVITY TIMES"
912   PRINT
920   PRINT "PREDECESSOR", "SUCCESSOR", "ACTUAL TIME", "MAXIMUM TIME"
921   PRINT

930   FOR I = 1 TO N2
931       LET N3 = P(I)
932       GOSUB 600
933       LET I1 = K
934       LET N3 = S(I)
935       GOSUB 600
936       LET I2 = K
937       LET D = L(I2) - E(I1)
938       IF T(I) = D THEN 941
939       PRINT P(I), S(I), T(I), D
940       GO TO 942
941       PRINT P(I), S(I), T(I), D, "CRITICAL PATH"
942   NEXT I
950   RETURN
```

Data

```
 999    REMARK -- TEST DATA FOR BCP

1000    REMARK -- EVENT NUMBERS
1001    DATA 10, 50, 20, 30, 15, 40, -1

1010    REMARK -- ACTIVITY DATA
1011    DATA 10, 20, 5
1020    DATA 10, 15, 7
1030    DATA 15, 20, 2
1040    DATA 15, 40, 18
1050    DATA 20, 30, 4
1060    DATA 30, 40, 4
1070    DATA 30, 50, 9
1080    DATA 40, 50, 6
1090    DATA -1, -1, -1
```

Output

```
                    EVENT TIMES

       EVENT      EARLIEST TIME   LATEST TIME

        10           0.0             0.0      CRITICAL PATH
        50            31              31      CRITICAL PATH
        20             9              17
        30            13              21
        15             7               7      CRITICAL PATH
        40            25              25      CRITICAL PATH

                    ACTIVITY TIMES

  PREDECESSOR    SUCCESSOR      ACTUAL TIME    MAXIMUM TIME

        10           20              5             17
        10           15              7              7      CRITICAL PATH
        15           20              2             10
        15           40             18             18      CRITICAL PATH
        20           30              4             12
        30           40              4             12
        30           50              9             18
        40           50              6              6      CRITICAL PATH
```

Grading (BGP)

Description

BGP converts students' scores on examinations to standardized scores based on the average score and the standard deviation of scores for the class as a whole. Scores are standardized to have a mean of seventy and a standard deviation of ten and are then rounded to the nearest tenth of a point. Each student's total score is computed by taking a weighted average of the standardized scores for the examinations he has taken. The percentage of the class above him and the percentage below him are also shown for each examination and for the total score. Finally, the program provides the instructor a list of student numbers and total scores in order (highest score first, lowest score last). The average score and standard deviation of scores for each examination are also provided.

Inputs

Inputs for a course must be provided in the following order:

Course number

Number of students in the class ($< = 100$)

Number of examinations given ($< = 10$)

Weight for examination one
.
.
.
Weight for last examination

Student number of first student
Score on examination one for first student
.
.
.
Score on last examination for first student

Student number of second student
Score on examination one for second student
.
.
.
Score on last examination for second student

.
.
.

Student number of last student ⎫
Score on examination one for last student ⎪
. ⎪
. ⎬
. ⎪
Score on last examination for last student ⎭

If a student did not take an examination, enter a minus number instead of the relevant score.

Additional courses may be analyzed; the inputs described above are simply repeated.

Method

BGP is primarily an exercise in data processing. The only features that might prove confusing are contained in subroutine 500, which arranges and prints total scores in order. The method for ranking uses a list (R) as follows: R(I) is intended to contain the (internal) number of the I-th–ranked student in the class. Initially the numbers of students for whom total scores have been calculated are loaded into list R in numeric order. Then a sorting procedure is followed to arrange the entires in R in the proper order. When the grades of an adjacent pair are not in the correct sequence, only the entries in list R are interchanged (this minimizes the movement of data). The other modification from the sorting technique described in the text concerns the limit of the entries tested. The sorting procedure utilized insures that, after the initial pass through the list, the correct item will be in the last position; after the second pass, the correct item will be in the next-to-last position; and so forth. Thus the pair-wise comparison is performed over one less position each time the list is processed.

Program

```
 5 REMARK -- GRADING PROGRAM

12 DIM G(100,10), D(100,10)

13 REMARK -- N0 IS THE NUMBER OF STUDENTS IN THE CLASS
14 REMARK -- N1 IS THE NUMBER OF EXAMS GIVEN
15 REMARK -- G(I,J) IS THE GRADE OF STUDENT I ON EXAM J
16 REMARK -- A MINUS GRADE INDICATES THAT THE STUDENT DID NOT TAKE THE EXAM
17 REMARK -- D(I,J) IS THE STANDARDIZED SCORE OF STUDENT I ON EXAM J
18 REMARK -- N(I) IS THE IDENTIFYING NUMBER OF STUDENT I
19 REMARK -- V(I) IS THE TOTAL WEIGHTED STANDARDIZED SCORE OF STUDENT I
20 REMARK -- A(J) IS THE AVERAGE SCORE ON EXAM J
21 REMARK -- S(J) IS THE STANDARD DEVIATION OF THE SCORES ON EXAM J
22 REMARK -- W(J) IS THE WEIGHT ASSIGNED TO EXAM J
23 REMARK -- Q(J) IS THE NUMBER OF STUDENTS WHO TOOK EXAM J
24 REMARK -- Q0 IS THE NUMBER OF STUDENTS WHO TOOK AT LEAST ONE EXAM

30 REMARK -- READ DATA
31 GOSUB 100

40 REMARK -- COMPUTE AVERAGES AND STANDARD DEVIATIONS
41 GOSUB 200

50 REMARK -- COMPUTE STANDARDIZED SCORES AND TOTAL SCORES
51 GOSUB 300

60 REMARK -- PRINT RESULTS
61 GOSUB 400

70 REMARK -- PRINT SUMMARY OF TOTAL SCORES
71 GOSUB 500

80 REMARK -- COURSE PROCESSED, GO TO NEXT SET OF DATA
81 GO TO 30
```

```
100 REMARK -- SUBROUTINE TO READ DATA
110 READ C
112 PRINT "GRADES FOR COURSE NUMBER ", C
113 PRINT
120 READ N0
121 PRINT "NUMBER OF STUDENTS IN CLASS =", N0
130 READ N1
131 PRINT "NUMBER OF EXAMS GIVEN =", N1
132 PRINT

140 FOR J = 1 TO N1
141     READ W(J)
142     PRINT "WEIGHT FOR EXAM", J, "        =", W(J)
143 NEXT J
144 PRINT

150 FOR I = 1 TO N0
151     READ N(I)
152     FOR J = 1 TO N1
153         READ G(I,J)
154     NEXT J
155 NEXT I
160 RETURN

200 REMARK -- SUBROUTINE TO COMPUTE AVERAGES AND STANDARD DEVIATIONS
210 FOR J = 1 TO N1

211     REMARK -- COMPUTE AVERAGE SCORE
212     LET T = 0
213     LET Q(J) = 0
214     FOR I = 1 TO N0
215         IF G(I,J) <  0 THEN 218
216         LET Q(J) = Q(J) + 1
217         LET T = T + G(I,J)
218     NEXT I
219     LET A(J) = T/Q(J)

220     REMARK -- COMPUTE STANDARD DEVIATION OF SCORES
221     LET T = 0
222     FOR I = 1 TO N0
223         IF G(I,J) <  0 THEN 225
224         LET T = T + ( (G(I,J) - A(J) )^2 )
225     NEXT I
226     LET S(J) = ( T/Q(J) )^.5

230     REMARK -- PRINT RESULTS
231     PRINT "EXAMINATION NUMBER", J
232     PRINT "AVERAGE =", A(J), "STD DEVIATION =", S(J)
233     PRINT Q(J), "STUDENTS TOOK THE EXAMINATION "
234     PRINT

235 NEXT J
240 RETURN
```

```
300 REMARK -- SUBROUTINE TO COMPUTE STANDARDIZED SCORES AND TOTAL SCORES

310 LET Q0 = 0
311 FOR I = 1 TO N0

312     REMARK -- COMPUTE STANDARDIZED SCORES
313     LET T = 0
314     LET T1 = 0
315     LET V(I) = 9999
316     FOR J = 1 TO N1
317         IF G(I,J) >= 0 THEN 320
318         LET D(I,J) = -1
319         GO TO 323

320         LET D(I,J) = .1 * INT( 700 + (100*(G(I,J)-A(J))/S(J) ) + .5 )
321         LET T = T + ( W(J) * D(I,J) )
322         LET T1 = T1 + W(J)

323     NEXT J

330     REMARK -- COMPUTE TOTAL SCORE
331     IF T = 0 THEN 340
332     LET V(I) = T / T1
333     LET Q0 = Q0 + 1

340 NEXT I

350 RETURN
```

```
400 REMARK -- SUBROUTINE TO PRINT RESULTS
401 PRINT

410 FOR I = 1 TO NO
420     PRINT "STUDENT NUMBER ", N(I)
421     PRINT "    EXAM", "   GRADE", "STD SCORE", "PCT ABOVE", "PCT BELOW"

430     REMARK -- PRINT EXAM SCORES
431     FOR J = 1 TO N1
432         IF G(I,J) >= 0 THEN 435
433         PRINT J, "NOT TAKEN"
434         GO TO 460

435         LET N3 = 0
436         LET N4 = 0
437         FOR K = 1 TO NO
438             IF G(K,J) >  G(I,J) THEN 441
439             IF G(K,J) <  G(I,J) THEN 443
440             GO TO 445
441             LET N3 = N3 + 1
442             GO TO 445
443             IF G(K,J) <  0 THEN 445
444             LET N4 = N4 + 1
445         NEXT K

450         LET P1 = INT( ( (N3/Q(J))*100) + .5)
451         LET P2 = INT( ( (N4/Q(J))*100) + .5)
452         PRINT J, G(I,J), D(I,J), P1, P2

460     NEXT J

469     IF N1 = 1 THEN 495
470     REMARK -- PRINT TOTAL SCORES
471     IF V(I) = 9999 THEN 495
481     LET N3 = 0
482     LET N4 = 0
483     FOR K = 1 TO NO
484         IF V(K) >  V(I) THEN 487
485         IF V(K) <  V(I) THEN 490
486         GO TO 491
487         IF V(K) = 9999 THEN 491
488         LET N3 = N3 + 1
489         GO TO 491
490         LET N4 = N4 + 1
491     NEXT K

492     LET P1 = INT ( ( (N3/Q0)*100) + .5)
493     LET P2 = INT ( ( (N4/Q0)*100) + .5)
494     PRINT " TOTAL SCORE", " " , V(I), P1, P2
495     PRINT

496 NEXT I
499 RETURN
```

```
500 REMARK -- SUBROUTINE TO PRINT SUMMARY OF TOTAL SCORES

510 REMARK -- LOAD LIST R
511 LET K = 0
512 FOR I = 1 TO N0
513     IF V(I) = 9999 THEN 516
514     LET K = K + 1
515     LET R(K) = I
516 NEXT I

520 REMARK -- RANK STUDENTS
521 LET N9 = 0
522 FOR K = 1 TO Q0-1
523     IF V(R(K)) >= V(R(K+1)) THEN 528
524     LET R1 = R(K)
525     LET R(K) = R(K+1)
526     LET R(K+1) = R1
527     LET N9 = 1
528 NEXT K
529 IF N9 = 1 THEN 521

530 REMARK -- PRINT SCORES
531 PRINT
532 PRINT "SUMMARY OF TOTAL SCORES"
533 PRINT
534 PRINT "    STUDENT", " TOTAL SCORE"
535 PRINT
536 FOR K = 1 TO Q0
537     PRINT N(R(K)), V(R(K))
538 NEXT K
539 RETURN
```

Data

```
 999    REMARK -- TEST DATA FOR BGP

1000    REMARK -- COURSE NUMBER
1001    DATA 301

1010    REMARK -- NUMBER OF STUDENTS
1011    DATA 10

1020    REMARK -- NUMBER OF EXAMS GIVEN
1021    DATA 3

1030    REMARK -- WEIGHTS
1031    DATA 1, 1, 2

1040    REMARK -- STUDENT DATA
1041    DATA 1, 80, 66, 88
1042    DATA 2, 90, 68, 95
1043    DATA 3, 68, 86, 65
1044    DATA 4, 75, 96, 67
1045    DATA 5, 63, -1, 59
1046    DATA 6, 95, 55, 46
1047    DATA 7, 57, 68, 95
1048    DATA 8, 66, 92, 76
1049    DATA 9, 48, 46, 49
1050    DATA 10, 89, 88, 99
```

Output

```
GRADES FOR COURSE NUMBER          301

NUMBER OF STUDENTS IN CLASS =      10
NUMBER OF EXAMS GIVEN =             3

WEIGHT FOR EXAM       1           =           1
WEIGHT FOR EXAM       2           =           1
WEIGHT FOR EXAM       3           =           2

EXAMINATION NUMBER                 1
AVERAGE =          73.1    STD DEVIATION =     14.6181
     10      STUDENTS TOOK THE EXAMINATION

EXAMINATION NUMBER                 2
AVERAGE =          73.8889  STD DEVIATION =    16.4279
      9      STUDENTS TOOK THE EXAMINATION

EXAMINATION NUMBER                 3
AVERAGE =          73.9    STD DEVIATION =     18.6304
     10      STUDENTS TOOK THE EXAMINATION


STUDENT NUMBER         1
    EXAM          GRADE        STD SCORE      PCT ABOVE      PCT BELOW
     1             80           74.7            30             60
     2             66           65.2            67             22
     3             88           77.6            30             60
 TOTAL SCORE                    73.775          20             70

STUDENT NUMBER         2
    EXAM          GRADE        STD SCORE      PCT ABOVE      PCT BELOW
     1             90           81.6            10             80
     2             68           66.4            44             33
     3             95           81.3            10             70
 TOTAL SCORE                    77.65           10             80

STUDENT NUMBER         3
    EXAM          GRADE        STD SCORE      PCT ABOVE      PCT BELOW
     1             68           66.5            50             40
     2             86           77.4            33             56
     3             65           65.2            60             30
 TOTAL SCORE                    68.575          60             30

STUDENT NUMBER         4
    EXAM          GRADE        STD SCORE      PCT ABOVE      PCT BELOW
     1             75           71.3            40             50
     2             96           83.5            0.0            89
     3             67           66.3            50             40
 TOTAL SCORE                    71.85           50             40
```

```
STUDENT NUMBER         5
    EXAM          GRADE        STD SCORE      PCT ABOVE      PCT BELOW
     1              63            63.1            70             20
     2          NOT TAKEN
     3              59            62              70             20
TOTAL SCORE                      62.3667         80             10

STUDENT NUMBER         6
    EXAM          GRADE        STD SCORE      PCT ABOVE      PCT BELOW
     1              95            85              0.0            90
     2              55            58.5            78             11
     3              46            55              90             0.0
TOTAL SCORE                      63.375          70             20

STUDENT NUMBER         7
    EXAM          GRADE        STD SCORE      PCT ABOVE      PCT BELOW
     1              57            59              80             10
     2              68            66.4            44             33
     3              95            81.3            10             70
TOTAL SCORE                      72              40             50

STUDENT NUMBER         8
    EXAM          GRADE        STD SCORE      PCT ABOVE      PCT BELOW
     1              66            65.1            60             30
     2              92            81              11             78
     3              76            71.1            40             50
TOTAL SCORE                      72.075          30             60

STUDENT NUMBER         9
    EXAM          GRADE        STD SCORE      PCT ABOVE      PCT BELOW
     1              48            52.8            90             0.0
     2              46            53              89             0.0
     3              49            56.6            80             10
TOTAL SCORE                      54.75           90             0.0

STUDENT NUMBER        10
    EXAM          GRADE        STD SCORE      PCT ABOVE      PCT BELOW
     1              89            80.9            20             70
     2              88            78.6            22             67
     3              99            83.5            0.0            90
TOTAL SCORE                      81.625          0.0            90
```

```
SUMMARY OF TOTAL SCORES

    STUDENT       TOTAL SCORE

      10            81.625
       2            77.65
       1            73.775
       8            72.075
       7            72
       4            71.85
       3            68.575
       6            63.375
       5            62.3667
       9            54.75
```

Questionnaire Analysis (BQA)

Description

BQA tabulates the answers to a series of questions provided on a set of questionnaires. As many as nine possible responses are allowed for each question. Responses are coded one through nine; a code of zero signifies no response. A questionnaire may include as many as a hundred different questions. The program summarizes the number of responses of each type for each of the questions (both in absolute and percentage terms). Moreover, as many as twenty-five cross-tabulations may be requested. Each cross-tabulation indicates the number (and percentage) of the respondents giving each of the possible pairs of responses to any two preselected questions.

Inputs

Number of questions ($<=100$)

Number of cross-tabulations ($<=25$)

First question
Second question } First cross-tabulation

.

.

.

First question
Second question } Last cross-tabulation

Response to question 1

.

.

.

Response to last question } First questionnaire

.

.

.

Response to question 1

.

.

.

Response to last question } Last questionnaire

99

Additional sets of questionnaires may be analyzed; the inputs described above are simply repeated.

Method

BQA is a somewhat mundane exercise in data processing, involving rather large amounts of data, relatively simple arithmetic, and slightly complicated output formats. The only challenge arises in connection with the cross-tabulation. The cumulative results are maintained in Table C. Each row contains the results of one of the requested cross-tabulations. One hundred columns (0 through 99) are provided—one for each possible pair of responses to the two questions. The relationship between the responses and the selected column is straightforward: the response to the first question is multiplied by 10 and added to the response to the second question (line 162). Later the process is reversed (lines 283 and 284), using the integer function. This procedure makes it possible to store information that logically requires a three-dimensional table (box?) in a two-dimensional table.

Program

```
  5  REMARK -- PROGRAM TO ANALYZE QUESTIONNAIRE RESPONSES

 10  DIM X(25), Y(25), R(100), C(25,99), T(100,9)

 11  REMARK -- X(I) IS THE FIRST QUESTION IN CROSS-TABULATION I
 12  REMARK -- Y(I) IS THE SECOND QUESTION IN CROSS-TABULATION I
 13  REMARK -- R(I) IS THE RESPONSE TO QUESTION I
 14  REMARK -- C(I,J) IS THE COUNT FOR RESPONSE COMBINATION J FOR CROSS-TAB I
 16  REMARK -- T(I,J) IS THE COUNT FOR RESPONSE J TO QUESTION I
 17  REMARK -- N1 IS THE NUMBER OF QUESTIONS
 18  REMARK -- N2 IS THE NUMBER OF CROSS-TABULATIONS
 19  REMARK -- N3 IS THE NUMBER OF QUESTIONNAIRES

 20  REMARK -- CLEAR VECTORS
 21  FOR I9 = 1 TO 25
 22     FOR J9 = 0 TO 99
 23        LET C(I9,J9) = 0
 24     NEXT J9
 25  NEXT I9

 26  FOR I9 = 1 TO 100
 27     FOR J9 = 0 TO 9
 28        LET T(I9,J9) = 0
 29     NEXT J9
 30  NEXT I9
 31  LET N3 = 0

 40  REMARK -- READ DATA AND ADD TO SUMS
 41  GOSUB 100

 50  REMARK -- PRINT RESULTS
 52  GOSUB 200

 60  REMARK -- DO A NEW PROBLEM
 61  GO TO 20
```

```
100    REMARK -- SUBROUTINE TO READ DATA AND ADD TO SUMS

110    REMARK -- READ NUMBER OF QUESTIONS
111    READ N1
112    IF N1 <= 100 THEN 120
113    PRINT "PROGRAM STOPPED -- I CAN ONLY HANDLE 100 QUESTIONS "
114    STOP

120    REMARK -- READ NUMBER OF CROSS-TABULATIONS
121    READ N2
122    IF N2 <= 25 THEN 130
123    PRINT "PROGRAM STOPPED -- I CAN ONLY HANDLE 25 CROSS-TABULATIONS"
124    STOP

130    REMARK -- READ IN QUESTIONS TO BE CROSS-TABULATED
131    FOR I9 = 1 TO N2
132      READ X(I9), Y(I9)
133    NEXT I9

140    REMARK -- READ RESPONSES FROM ONE QUESTIONNAIRE
141    FOR I9 = 1 TO N1
142      READ R9
143      IF R9 = 99 THEN 170
144      LET R(I9) = R9
145      IF R9 >  9 THEN 147
146      IF R9 >= 0 THEN 149
147      PRINT "PROGRAM STOPPED -- EACH RESPONSE MUST BE BETWEEN 0 AND 9"
148      STOP
149      LET T(I9,R9) = T(I9,R9) + 1
150    NEXT I9

160    REMARK -- ADD TO CROSS-TABULATION SUMS
161    FOR I9 = 1 TO N2
162      LET R9 =(10 * R(X(I9)))+ R(Y(I9))
163      LET C(I9,R9) = C(I9,R9) + 1
164    NEXT I9
165    LET N3 = N3 + 1
166    GO TO 140

170    RETURN
```

```
200   REMARK -- PRINT RESULTS

211   PRINT "NUMBER OF QUESTIONNAIRES = ", N3
212   PRINT

220   FOR I9 = 1 TO N1
221     PRINT "  RESPONSES TO QUESTION NUMBER", I9
222     PRINT "================================================="
223     PRINT "  RESPONSE", "    NUMBER", "    PERCENT"
224     IF T(I9,0) = 0 THEN 230
225     LET P9 = .1 * INT( (1000*T(I9,0)/N3) + .5 )
226     PRINT "    NONE", T(I9,0), P9
230     FOR J9 = 1 TO 9
231       LET T9 = T(I9,J9)
232       IF T9 = 0 THEN 235
233       LET P9 = .1 * INT( (1000*T9/N3) + .5 )
234       PRINT J9, T9, P9
235     NEXT J9
240     PRINT
241   NEXT I9

250   REMARK -- PRINT CROSS-TABULATIONS
260   FOR I9 = 1 TO N2
270     PRINT
271     PRINT "CROSS-TABULATION", I9
272     PRINT
273     PRINT "  RESPONSE TO", "  RESPONSE TO"
274     PRINT "    QUESTION", "    QUESTION"
275     PRINT X(I9), Y(I9), "    NUMBER", "    PERCENT"
276     PRINT "================================================================="

280     FOR J9 = 0 TO 99
281       LET C9 = C(I9,J9)
282       IF C9 = 0 THEN 295
283       LET R1 = INT(J9/10)
284       LET R2 = J9 - (10*R1)
285       IF R1 = 0 THEN 288
286       PRINT R1,
287       GO TO 289
288       PRINT "    NONE",
289       IF R2 = 0 THEN 292
290       PRINT R2,
291       GO TO 293
292       PRINT "    NONE",
293       LET P9 = .1 * INT( (1000*C9/N3) + .5 )
294       PRINT C9, P9
295     NEXT J9

298   NEXT I9
299   RETURN
```

Data

```
 999    REMARK -- TEST DATA FOR BQA

1000    REMARK -- NUMBER OF QUESTIONS
1001    DATA 3

1010    REMARK -- NUMBER OF CROSS-TABULATIONS
1011    DATA 2

1012    REMARK -- QUESTIONS TO BE CROSS-TABULATED
1013    DATA 1, 2
1014    DATA 1, 3

1020    REMARK -- QUESTIONNAIRE RESPONSES
1021    DATA 0, 2, 6
1022    DATA 2, 3, 5
1023    DATA 6, 7, 9
1024    DATA 2, 0, 7
1025    DATA 2, 3, 5
1026    DATA 3, 1, 5
1027    DATA 2, 3, 6
1028    DATA 99
```

Output

```
NUMBER OF QUESTIONNAIRES =           7
   RESPONSES TO QUESTION NUMBER         1
==========================================
   RESPONSE        NUMBER        PERCENT
     NONE            1            14.3
      2              4            57.1
      3              1            14.3
      6              1            14.3

   RESPONSES TO QUESTION NUMBER         2
==========================================
   RESPONSE        NUMBER        PERCENT
     NONE            1            14.3
      1              1            14.3
      2              1            14.3
      3              3            42.9
      7              1            14.3

   RESPONSES TO QUESTION NUMBER         3
==========================================
   RESPONSE        NUMBER        PERCENT
      5              3            42.9
      6              2            28.6
      7              1            14.3
      9              1            14.3


CROSS-TABULATION                     1

   RESPONSE TO    RESPONSE TO
   QUESTION       QUESTION
      1              2          NUMBER       PERCENT
==============================================================
     NONE            2            1           14.3
      2             NONE          1           14.3
      2              3            3           42.9
      3              1            1           14.3
      6              7            1           14.3

CROSS-TABULATION                     2

   RESPONSE TO    RESPONSE TO
   QUESTION       QUESTION
      1              3          NUMBER       PERCENT
==============================================================
     NONE            6            1           14.3
      2              5            2           28.6
      2              6            1           14.3
      2              7            1           14.3
      3              5            1           14.3
      6              9            1           14.3
```

Regression and Correlation (BRC)

Description

BRC performs simple regression and correlation analyses on a series of observations of the values of two variables. The correlation coefficient between the variables is computed, and up to four regression equations are estimated, using the method of least-squares. The four equations are

1. Variable $2 = a + b$ (variable 1)
2. Variable $2 = a + b$ (natural log of variable 1)
3. Natural log of variable $2 = a + b$ (variable 1)
4. Natural log of variable $2 = a + b$ (natural log of variable 1)

If any observation contains a negative or zero value of one of the variables, the equations using the natural log of that variable are not estimated.

Coefficients for each equation are chosen to minimize the deviations of the actual values of the quantity to the left of the equal sign (above) from the estimated values. However, the extent to which the equation fits the data is indicated by the percentage of the variation in variable 2 that is explained by the equation. Equations 3 and 4 are presented both in the forms shown above and in alternate forms in which variable 2 is the dependent variable. The program also gives the average value and standard deviation of values for each variable.

Inputs

Number of observations ($< = 500$)

Variable 1 ⎫
Variable 2 ⎬ First observation

.

.

.

Variable 1 ⎫
Variable 2 ⎬ Last observation

Several problems may be solved; the inputs described above are simply repeated for each problem.

Method

The program uses the standard method of least-squares. The regression analysis is performed in subroutine 500, which regresses values of $B(I)$ on values of $A(I)$. The main program uses the values of the actual variables stored in X(I) and Y(I) to prepare the values in A(I) and B(I) before calling in subroutine 500. The remainder of the program performs input and output and supplementary calculations.

Program

```
10      REMARK -- REGRESSION AND CORRELATION PROGRAM

20      REMARK -- READ DATA
21      GOSUB 200

30      REMARK -- REGRESS VARIABLE 2 ON VARIABLE 1
31      FOR I = 1 TO N
32          LET A(I) = X(I)
33          LET B(I) = Y(I)
34      NEXT I
35      GOSUB 500

40      REMARK -- PRINT AVERAGES AND STANDARD DEVIATIONS
41      PRINT
42      PRINT "THE AVERAGE VALUE OF VARIABLE 1 IS", A1
43      PRINT "THE AVERAGE VALUE OF VARIABLE 2 IS", A2
44      PRINT "THE STANDARD DEVIATION OF VARIABLE 1 IS", D1
45      PRINT "THE STANDARD DEVIATION OF VARIABLE 2 IS", D2
46      PRINT "THE CORRELATION COEFFICIENT BETWEEN VARIABLES 1 AND 2 IS", C9
47      LET A9 = A2

50      PRINT
51      PRINT "EQUATION 1"
52      PRINT " VARIABLE 2 =", I9, "        +", S9, "* VARIABLE 1"
53      PRINT P9, "PERCENT OF THE VARIANCE IN VARIABLE 2 EXPLAINED"
54      PRINT

60      REMARK -- REGRESS VARIABLE 2 ON LOG OF VARIABLE 1
61      FOR I = 1 TO N
62          IF X(I) <= 0 THEN 80
63          LET A(I) = LOG(X(I))
64      NEXT I
65      GOSUB 500
66      PRINT "EQUATION 2"
67      PRINT "VARIABLE 2 =", I9, "        +", S9, "*LOG OF VAR 1 "
68      PRINT P9, "PERCENT OF THE VARIANCE IN VARIABLE 2 EXPLAINED "
69      PRINT

80      REMARK -- REGRESS LOG OF VAR 2 ON VAR 1
81      FOR I = 1 TO N
82          LET A(I) = X(I)
83          IF Y(I) <= 0 THEN 20
84          LET B(I) = LOG(Y(I))
85      NEXT I
86      GOSUB 500
87      GOSUB 600
88      PRINT "EQUATION 3"
89      PRINT "LOG(VAR 2) =", I9, "     +", S9, "* VARIABLE 1"
90      PRINT "ALTERNATE FORM --"
91      PRINT "VARIABLE 2 =", EXP(I9), "        *", EXP(S9), "↑ VAR 1"
92      PRINT P9, "PERCENT OF THE VARIANCE IN VARIABLE 2 EXPLAINED "
93      PRINT
```

```
100     REMARK -- REGRESS LOG OF VAR 2 ON LOG OF VAR 1
101     FOR I = 1 TO N
102        IF A(I) <= 0 THEN 20
103        LET A(I) = LOG(X(I))
104     NEXT I
105     GOSUB 500
106     GOSUB 600
107     PRINT "EQUATION 4"
108     PRINT "LOG(VAR 2) =", I9, "        +", S9, "*LOG(VAR 1)"
109     PRINT "ALTERNATE FORM --"
110     PRINT "VARIABLE 2 =", EXP(I9), "* (VAR 1 ↑ ", S9, ")"
111     PRINT P9, "PERCENT OF THE VARIANCE IN VARIABLE 2 EXPLAINED"
120     GO TO 20

200     REMARK -- SUBROUTINE TO READ DATA
201     READ N
202     PRINT
203     PRINT " ", "     DATA "
204     PRINT
205     PRINT " OBSERVATION", " VARIABLE 1", " VARIABLE 2"
206     PRINT
207     FOR I = 1 TO N
208        READ X(I), Y(I)
209        PRINT I, X(I), Y(I)
210     NEXT I
211     RETURN
```

```
500     REMARK -- SUBROUTINE TO REGRESS N VALUES OF B(I) ON A(I)

510     REMARK -- COMPUTE SUMS
511     LET S1 = 0
512     LET S2 = 0
513     LET S3 = 0
514     LET S4 = 0
515     LET S5 = 0
516     FOR I = 1 TO N
517         LET S1 = S1 + A(I)
518         LET S2 = S2 + B(I)
519         LET S3 = S3 + ( A(I)↑2 )
520         LET S4 = S4 + ( B(I)↑2 )
521         LET S5 = S5 + ( A(I)*B(I) )
522     NEXT I

530     REMARK -- COMPUTE AVERAGES
531     LET A1 = S1/N
532     LET A2 = S2/N

535     REMARK -- COMPUTE VARIANCES
536     LET V1 = ( S3 -(N*(A1↑2)) )/(N-1)
537     LET V2 = ( S4 - (N*(A2↑2)) )/(N-1)

540     REMARK -- COMPUTE STANDARD DEVIATIONS
541     LET D1 = SQR(V1)
542     LET D2 = SQR(V2)

550     REMARK -- COMPUTE DIVISOR FOR REGRESSION LINE
551     LET D0 = (N*S3) - (S1↑2)
552     REMARK -- COMPUTE INTERCEPT (I9) AND SLOPE (S9)
553     LET I9 = ( (S2*S3) - (S1*S5) )/D0
554     LET S9 = ( (N*S5) - (S1*S2) ) /D0

560     REMARK -- COMPUTE PERCENT OF VARIANCE EXPLAINED (P9)
561     LET P9 = ( (S9↑2)*V1) / V2

570     REMARK -- COMPUTE CORRELATION COEFFICIENT (C9)
571     LET C9 = SQR(P9)
572     LET P9 = 100 * P9
580     RETURN
```

ΣX

ΣY

ΣX^2

ΣY^2

ΣXY

$$\frac{\Sigma X^2 - N(\Sigma X)^2}{N-1}$$

$$\frac{\Sigma Y^2 - N(\Sigma Y)^2}{N-1}$$

$$N\Sigma X^2 - (\Sigma X)^2$$

$$\frac{\Sigma Y \Sigma X^2 - \Sigma X \Sigma XY}{N\Sigma X^2 - (\Sigma X)^2} = A$$

$$\frac{N\Sigma XY - \Sigma X \Sigma Y}{N\Sigma X^2 - (\Sigma X)^2} = B.$$

$$Y = A + BX$$

% var explained: $r^2 = \frac{(B)^2 V_x}{V_y}$

$$r = \left(\frac{B \sqrt{V_x}}{\sqrt{V_y}} \right) 100$$

```
600     REMARK -- SUBROUTINE TO FIND PERCENT OF VARIANCE IN VAR 2 EXPLAINED
601     LET S8 = 0
602     LET S7 = 0
603     FOR I = 1 TO N
604         LET E = EXP( I9 +(S9*A(I)))
605         LET S8 = S8 + ( (Y(I)-E)↑2 )
606         LET S7 = S7 + ( (Y(I)-A9)↑2 )
607     NEXT I
608     LET P9 = 100 * ( 1 - (S8/S7) )
609     RETURN
```

Data

```
999     REMARK -- TEST DATA FOR BRC

1000    REMARK -- NUMBER OF OBSERVATIONS
1001    DATA 5

1010    REMARK -- DATA
1011    DATA 10, 20
1012    DATA 15, 30
1013    DATA 5, 40
1014    DATA 40, 20
1015    DATA 20, 20
```

Output

```
                    DATA

   OBSERVATION     VARIABLE 1      VARIABLE 2

        1              10             20
        2              15             30
        3               5             40
        4              40             20
        5              20             20

THE AVERAGE VALUE OF VARIABLE 1 IS                   18
THE AVERAGE VALUE OF VARIABLE 2 IS                   26
THE STANDARD DEVIATION OF VARIABLE 1 IS              13.5093
THE STANDARD DEVIATION OF VARIABLE 2 IS              8.94427
THE CORRELATION COEFFICIENT BETWEEN VARIABLES 1 AND 2 IS        .600014

EQUATION 1
 VARIABLE 2 =          33.1507           +              -.39726 * VARIABLE 1
      36.0017  PERCENT OF THE VARIANCE IN VARIABLE 2 EXPLAINED

EQUATION 2
 VARIABLE 2 =          48.7463           +              -8.54823 *LOG OF VAR 1
      54.9193  PERCENT OF THE VARIANCE IN VARIABLE 2 EXPLAINED

EQUATION 3
 LOG(VAR 2) =          3.46764          +              -.01401 * VARIABLE 1
 ALTERNATE FORM --
 VARIABLE 2 =          32.0608          *              .986088 ↑ VAR 1
      37.1992  PERCENT OF THE VARIANCE IN VARIABLE 2 EXPLAINED

EQUATION 4
 LOG(VAR 2) =          4.00071          +              -.295105 *LOG(VAR 1)
 ALTERNATE FORM --
 VARIABLE 2 =          54.637   * (VAR 1 ↑            -.295105 )
      58.0933  PERCENT OF THE VARIANCE IN VARIABLE 2 EXPLAINED
```

Simultaneous Linear Equations (BSLE)

Description

BSLE finds the set of values of N variables consistent with a set of N (simultaneous) linear equations. If no solution exists an appropriate message is printed.

Inputs

Inputs for a problem must be provided in the following order:

Number of variables ($< = 50$)

$$\left.\begin{array}{l}\text{Equation number}\\\text{Variable number}\\\text{Coefficient}\end{array}\right\}\text{First nonzero coefficient}$$

$$\left.\begin{array}{l}\text{Equation number}\\\text{Variable number}\\\text{Coefficient}\end{array}\right\}\text{Second nonzero coefficient}$$

$$\vdots$$

$$\left.\begin{array}{l}\text{Equation number}\\\text{Variable number}\\\text{Coefficient}\end{array}\right\}\text{Last nonzero coefficient}$$

$$\begin{array}{l}-1\\-1\\-1\end{array}$$

Right-hand sides (constants) are indicated by specifying a variable number of 99.

Additional problems may be solved; the inputs described above are simply repeated.

Method

The program uses the Gaussian elimination method. The coefficients are placed in a table with N rows and $N + 1$ columns (where N is the number of variables and also the number of equations). Simple algebraic manipulations are then applied to obtain a table with zeros in the bottom-left triangle and ones down the diagonal, since the solution can easily be calculated from such a table. Dividing a row by the value in any given column gives a one in the desired position. Subtracting such a row from another with a one in the same column gives a row with a zero in the column in question. These relationships make it possible to proceed from the top row to the bottom row until the desired table is obtained. If at some point a row cannot be altered as desired, some subsequent row is utilized instead (if no satisfactory row can be found there is no solution to the problem). Once the desired table is found, the values of the variables are readily computed, starting with the last (N-th) variable and working backwards.

Program

```
10    REMARK - PROGRAM TO SOLVE SIMULTANEOUS LINEAR EQUATIONS

11    DIM A(50,51)

13    REMARK - INPUT DATA
14    GOSUB 100

15    REMARK - SET UP TABLE
16    GOSUB 200
17    IF Z5 = 1 THEN 13

18    REMARK - FIND VALUES OF VARIABLES
19    GOSUB 300

20    REMARK - PRINT SOLUTION
21    GOSUB 400

22    GO TO 13

100   REMARK - SUBROUTINE TO READ DATA
101   PAGE
102   READ N
103   PRINT "NUMBER OF VARIABLES =", N
104   REMARK - SET ALL VALUES TO ZERO
105   FOR I = 1 TO N
106       FOR J = 1 TO N+1
107           LET A(I,J) = 0
108       NEXT J
109   NEXT I

110   PRINT
111   PRINT"   EQUATION", "   VARIABLE", "COEFFICIENT"
112   PRINT

113   REMARK - READ A VALUE
114   READ I, J, X
115   IF I <= 0 THEN 130
116   REMARK -- THIS IS NOT THE LAST SET (LAST SET HAS THREE -1"S)
117   IF J = 99 THEN 121
118   PRINT I, J, X
119   LET A(I,J) = X
120   GO TO 113
121   PRINT I, "RIGHT-HAND SIDE", X
122   LET A(I,N+1) = X
123   GO TO 113

130   REMARK - ALL VALUES INPUT
131   LET Z5 = 0
132   RETURN
```

```
200   REMARK - SUBROUTINE TO SET UP TABLE
201   REMARK - PROCESS EACH ROW (I)
202   FOR I = 1 TO N
203       LET N1 = 0
204       REMARK - PROCESS EACH COLUMN (K) THROUGH I-1
205       FOR K = 1 TO I-1
206           LET E = A(I,K)
207           REMARK -- IF E IS ALREADY ZERO, GO AHEAD
208           IF E = 0 THEN 217
209           REMARK - DIVIDE BY E TO GET 1 IN COLUMN K
210           FOR L = K TO N+1
211               LET A(I,L) = A(I,L) / E
212           NEXT L
213           REMARK - SUBTRACT THIS ROW FROM ROW K
214           FOR L = K TO N+1
215               LET A(I,L) = A(K,L) - A(I,L)
216           NEXT L
217       NEXT K
218       REMARK - PUT 1 IN COLUMN I
219       LET E = A(I,I)
220       REMARK -- IF E IS ZERO, SWITCH ROWS
221       IF E = 0 THEN 250
222       FOR L = I TO N+1
223           LET A(I,L) = A(I,L) / E
224       NEXT L
225       REMARK - THIS ROW IS ALL SET
226       GO TO 290

250       REMARK - A DIAGONAL ELEMENT WAS ZERO - CHECK FOR NO SOLUTION
251       IF N1 = N - I THEN 500
252       LET N1 = N1 + 1
253       REMARK - STORE THIS ROW IN S
254       FOR L = 1 TO N+1
255           LET S(L) = A(I,L)
256       NEXT L
257       REMARK - MOVE ALL SUBSEQUENT ROWS UP
258       FOR M = I+1 TO N
259           FOR L = 1 TO N+1
260               LET A(M-1,L) = A(M,L)
261           NEXT L
262       NEXT M
263       REMARK - PUT ROW I AT BOTTOM
264       FOR L = 1 TO N+1
265           LET A(N,L) = S(L)
266       NEXT L
267       REMARK - TRY AGAIN
268       GO TO 204

290       REMARK - CONTINUE WITH THE NEXT ROW
291   NEXT I
292   REMARK - TABLE IS ALL SET
293   RETURN
```

```
300  REMARK - SUBROUTINE TO FIND VALUES OF VARIABLES
301  FOR I = N TO 1 STEP -1
302      LET X(I) = A(I,N+1)
303      FOR J = I+1 TO N
304          LET X(I) = X(I) - ( A(I,J) * X(J) )
305      NEXT J
306  NEXT I
307  RETURN

400  REMARK - SUBROUTINE TO PRINT SOLUTION
401  PRINT
402  PRINT "SOLUTION"
403  PRINT
404  PRINT "   VARIABLE", "    VALUE "
405  PRINT
406  FOR I = 1 TO N
407      PRINT I, X(I)
408  NEXT I
409  RETURN

500  REMARK - THIS POINT REACHED IF NO SOLUTION CAN BE FOUND
501  PRINT
502  PRINT " SORRY - NO SOLUTION "
503  LET Z5 = 1
504  RETURN
```

Data

```
 999     REMARK -- TEST DATA FOR BSLE

1000     REMARK -- NUMBER OF VARIABLES
1001     DATA 3

1010     REMARK -- COEFFICIENTS
1011     DATA 1, 1, 2
1012     DATA 1, 2, 3
1013     DATA 1, 3, -1
1014     DATA 1, 99, 20
1015     DATA 2, 3, 1
1016     DATA 2, 99, 5
1017     DATA 3, 1, 1
1018     DATA 3, 3, -1
1019     DATA 3, 99, 3
1020     DATA -1, -1, -1
```

Output

```
NUMBER OF VARIABLES =              3

   EQUATION        VARIABLE    COEFFICIENT

      1               1             2
      1               2             3
      1               3            -1
      1        RIGHT-HAND SIDE     20
      2               3             1
      2        RIGHT-HAND SIDE      5
      3               1             1
      3               3            -1
      3        RIGHT-HAND SIDE      3

SOLUTION

   VARIABLE          VALUE

      1               8
      2               3
      3               5
```

Subroutines for Automatic File Maintenance (BSAFM)

Description

BSAFM includes a set of subroutines that can be used whenever automatic file maintenance is desired. A *record* is composed of one or more *items* (numbers). A *file* consists of a set of records. BSAFM allows you to use a single table to store the records contained in many separate files. Whenever a record is removed from a file, the space it occupied becomes available automatically for other files. Whenever you wish to place a record in a file, empty space is found and the record inserted. Moreover, you may specify the *file discipline* for each file (i.e., what rules are to be followed when inserting a new record). The available disciplines are as follows:

1. Push-down: the new record is inserted at the top (beginning) of the file.
2. Add-to-the-bottom: the new record is inserted at the bottom (end) of the file.
3. Rank in ascending order: records are maintained with the record containing the lowest-valued item first (at the top or beginning of the file) and the record containing the highest-valued item last (at the bottom or end of the file). In case of ties, the first record inserted comes first and the last record inserted comes last. The item number to be used for such a file is specified as part of the discipline.
4. Rank in descending order: similar to (3), except that the record containing the highest-valued item is first and that containing the lowest-valued item is last.

The technique used by BSAFM is sometimes called dynamic storage allocation, since storage is assigned and released as the program proceeds. The method uses list-processing techniques to minimize data transfers (see page 129).

Use

The subroutines use statement numbers ranging from 5100 through 5814; all variables begin with U, V, or W. Only four statements must be modified to suit the particular application: numbers 5111 through 5114. Instructions for modification are given in statements 5101 through 5104.

To initialize the system:

GOSUB 5100

To declare a file as push-down, place the file number in W1 and call subroutine 5200:

$$\text{LET W1} = 1$$
$$\text{GOSUB 5200}$$

To declare a file as add-to-bottom, place the file number in W1 and call subroutine 5300:

$$\text{LET W1} = \text{J}$$
$$\text{GOSUB 5300}$$

To declare a file as ranked in ascending order, place the file number in W1 and the item number to be used for the ranking in W2, and then call subroutine 5400:

$$\text{LET W1} = 2$$
$$\text{LET W2} = 1$$
$$\text{GOSUB 5400}$$

To declare a file as ranked in descending order, place the file number in W1 and the item number to be used for the ranking in W2, and then call subroutine 5500:

$$\text{LET W1} = 2$$
$$\text{LET W2} = 3$$
$$\text{GOSUB 5500}$$

To insert a record, place item 1 in V(1), item 2 in V(2), and so on. Then set W1 equal to the desired file number and GOSUB 5600:

$$\text{FOR I} = 1 \text{ TO N}$$
$$\text{LET V(I)} = \text{X(I)}$$
$$\text{NEXT I}$$
$$\text{LET W1} = 5$$
$$\text{GOSUB 5600}$$

To remove the top record from a file, simply specify the file number (W1) and call subroutine 5700:

$$\text{LET W1} = 4$$
$$\text{GOSUB 5700}$$

V(1) will contain the value of item 1 for the record removed, V(2) will contain the value of item 2, and so on. If no records remained in the file, V(0) will equal -1; otherwise it will be zero.

File discipline is utilized only when records are inserted. The discipline used for any file may thus be changed during the execution of the program if desired.

If at any time an attempt is made to insert a record when no space remains in the file system, a message is printed and execution stopped.

Statements 10 through 80 are included to demonstrate the use of the subroutines; in actual use they would be replaced by the user's own program.

Method

The method utilized is known as list processing. Records are kept in Table W, one record per row. Column 1 is used for item 1, column 2 for item 2, and so on. Column 0 is used to indicate the row in Table W where the next record in the file of which the record is a member is located. If the record is the last one in a file, column 0 contains a zero. A separate table is used to record the row containing the first record in each file. $U(W1,0)$ contains the row number of the row in Table W where the first record in file W1 is located. $U(W1,1)$ indicates the file discipline for file W1: 0 for push-down, 500 for add-to-bottom, W2 if ranked on item W2 in ascending order, and $-W2$ if ranked on item W2 in descending order. If file W1 is empty, $U(W1,0) = 0$.

Records not in a regular file are in the *empty file*. This is a push-down file maintained in the same manner as any regular file. $U(0,0)$ indicates the row containing the first record in the empty file, and each record "points" to the next record (except the last, which contains a zero in column 0).

When a record is to be inserted, the items are placed in the row currently containing the first record in the empty file. Then the pointers (column 0) of at most two of the other records in the file (W1) are altered to provide the appropriate links. $U(0,0)$ is also altered to point to the row containing the record that was formerly second in the empty file.

When a record is to be removed the items are placed in list V, the row is "returned" to the top of the empty file, and the value in $U(W1,0)$ is altered to point to the row containing the record that was formerly second in file W1.

When a record is to be inserted, the records in the appropriate file are checked in order by following the pointers from record to record until the correct location for insertion is found. The push-down discipline thus requires the least time for insertion and the add-to-bottom discipline the greatest. The time required to remove a record is minimal and is not, of course, affected by the file discipline.

Program

```
10      REMARK -- PROGRAM TO TEST THE BSAFM SYSTEM

11      REMARK -- INITIALIZE THE SYSTEM
12         GOSUB 5100
13      REMARK -- DECLARE FILE 1 AS PUSH-DOWN
14         LET W1 = 1
15         GOSUB 5200
16      REMARK -- DECLARE FILE 2 AS ADD-TO-BOTTOM
17         LET W1 = 2
18         GOSUB 5300
19      REMARK -- DECLARE FILE 3 AS RANKED ON ITEM 2 IN ASCENDING ORDER
20         LET W1 = 3
21         LET W2 = 2
22         GOSUB 5400
23      REMARK -- DECLARE FILE 4 AS RANKED ON ITEM 3 IN DESCENDING ORDER
24         LET W1 = 4
25         LET W2 = 3
26         GOSUB 5500

30      REMARK -- READ IN 5 RECORDS, EACH WITH 3 ITEMS
31      REMARK -- FILE EACH RECORD IN EACH OF THE FOUR FILES
40      FOR I = 1 TO 5
41         READ V(1), V(2), V(3)
42         REMARK -- FILE IN FILE 1
43            LET W1 = 1
44            GOSUB 5600
45         REMARK -- FILE IN FILE 2
46            LET W1 = 2
47            GOSUB 5600
48         REMARK -- FILE IN FILE 3
49            LET W1 = 3
50            GOSUB 5600
51         REMARK -- FILE IN FILE 4
52            LET W1 = 4
53            GOSUB 5600
54      NEXT I

60      REMARK -- PRINT THE CONTENTS OF EACH FILE
61      FOR W1 = 1 TO 4
62         PRINT "FILE", W1
63         PRINT
64         FOR I = 1 TO 5
65            GOSUB 5700
66            PRINT V(1), V(2), V(3)
67         NEXT I
68         PRINT
69         PRINT
70      NEXT W1
80      STOP
```

```
5100    REMARK -- SUBROUTINE TO INITIALIZE THE FILE SYSTEM
5101        REMARK -- V7 IS THE NUMBER OF ITEMS PER RECORD
5102        REMARK -- V8 IS THE MAXIMUM NUMBER OF RECORDS
5103        REMARK -- V9 IS THE NUMBER OF FILES
5104        REMARK -- DIMENSIONS ARE W(V8,V7), V(V7), U(V9,1)
5110    REMARK -- THE NEXT FOUR STATEMENTS MAY BE CHANGED AS DESIRED
5111        LET V7 = 3
5112        LET V8 = 100
5113        LET V9 = 10
5114        DIM W(100,3), V(3), U(10,1)
5120    REMARK -- CLEAR U
5121        FOR W4 = 0 TO V9
5122            FOR W3 = 0 TO 1
5123                LET U(W4,W3) = 0
5124            NEXT W3
5125        NEXT W4
5130    REMARK -- SET UP THE EMPTY LIST
5131        LET U(0,0) = 1
5132        FOR W4 = 1 TO V8-1
5133            LET W(W4,0) = W4 + 1
5134        NEXT W4
5140    RETURN

5200    REMARK -- SUBROUTINE TO DECLARE FILE W1 AS PUSH-DOWN
5201    LET U(W1,1) = 0
5202    RETURN

5300    REMARK -- SUBROUTINE TO DECLARE FILE W1 AS ADD-TO-BOTTOM
5301    LET U(W1,1) = 500
5302    RETURN

5400    REMARK - SUBROUTINE TO DECLARE FILE W1 RANKED ON W2 IN ASCENDING ORDER
5401    LET U(W1,1) = W2
5402    RETURN

5500    REMARK - SUBROUTINE TO DECLARE FILE W1 RANKED ON W2 IN DESCENDING ORDER
5501    LET U(W1,1) = -W2
5502    RETURN
```

```
5600    REMARK -- SUBROUTINE TO INSERT A RECORD IN FILE W1
5601      GOSUB 5800
5602      IF U(W1,0) = 0 THEN 5620
5603      IF U(W1,1) = 0 THEN 5620
5604      IF U(W1,1) = 500 THEN 5630
5605      IF U(W1,1) <  0 THEN 5609
5606      LET W2 = U(W1,1)
5607      LET W9 = 0
5608      GO TO 5650
5609      LET W2 = -U(W1,1)
5610      LET W9 = 1
5611      GO TO 5650
5620    REMARK -- INSERT THE RECORD AT THE BEGINNING OF FILE W1
5621      LET W(V5,0) = U(W1,0)
5622      LET U(W1,0) = V5
5623      RETURN
5630    REMARK -- INSERT THE RECORD AT THE END OF FILE W1
5631      LET W6 = 0
5632      LET V4 = U(W1,0)
5633      IF W(V4,0) = 0 THEN 5640
5634      LET V4 = W(V4,0)
5635      LET W6 = W6 + 1
5636      IF W6 <= V8 THEN 5633
5637      PRINT "SORRY -- THE FILE IS ALL MESSED UP"
5638      STOP
5640      LET W(V4,0) = V5
5641      LET W(V5,0) = 0
5642      RETURN
5650    REMARK -- INSERT THE RECORD RANKED ON ITEM W2
5651      LET V2 = W(V5,W2)
5652      LET V3 = 0
5653      LET V4 = U(W1,0)
5654      IF W9 = 1 THEN 5657
5655      IF W(V4,W2) >  V2 THEN 5670
5656      GO TO 5658
5657      IF W(V4,W2) <  V2 THEN 5670
5658      IF W(V4,0) = 0 THEN 5680
5659      LET V3 = V4
5660      LET V4 = W(V4,0)
5661      GO TO 5654
5670    REMARK -- INSERT V5 BETWEEN V3 AND V4
5671      IF V3 = 0 THEN 5620
5672      LET W(V3,0) = V5
5673      LET W(V5,0) = V4
5674      RETURN
5680    REMARK -- INSERT AFTER V4
5681      LET W(V4,0) = V5
5682      LET W(V5,0) = 0
5683      RETURN
```

```
5700    REMARK -- SUBROUTINE TO REMOVE FIRST ITEM FROM FILE W1
5701       IF U(W1,0) = 0 THEN 5720
5702       LET V5 = U(W1,0)
5703       LET U(W1,0) = W(V5,0)
5704       FOR W4 = 1 TO V7
5705          LET V(W4) = W(V5,W4)
5706       NEXT W4
5707       LET W(V5,0) = U(0,0)
5708       LET U(0,0) = V5
5709       LET V(0) = 0
5710       RETURN
5720    REMARK -- NOTHING IN FILE W1
5721       LET V(0) = -1
5722       RETURN

5800    REMARK -- SUBROUTINE TO INSERT A RECORD -- LOCATION WILL BE V5
5801       LET V5 = U(0,0)
5802       IF W(V5,0) <> 0 THEN 5810
5803       PRINT "SORRY -- TOO MANY RECORDS"
5804       STOP
5810       LET U(0,0) = W(V5,0)
5811       FOR W4 = 1 TO V7
5812          LET W(V5,W4) = V(W4)
5813       NEXT W4
5814       RETURN
```

Data

```
9000    REMARK -- TEST DATA FOR BSAFM
9001    REMARK -- EACH DATA LINE IS A RECORD OF THREE ITEMS

9002    DATA 10, 10, 10
9003    DATA 10, 20, 30
9004    DATA 30, 20, 10
9005    DATA 90, 40, 10
9006    DATA 80, 10, 90
```

Output

```
FILE                    1

        80          10          90
        90          40          10
        30          20          10
        10          20          30
        10          10          10


FILE                    2

        10          10          10
        10          20          30
        30          20          10
        90          40          10
        80          10          90


FILE                    3

        10          10          10
        80          10          90
        10          20          30
        30          20          10
        90          40          10


FILE                    4

        80          10          90
        10          20          30
        10          10          10
        30          20          10
        90          40          10
```

A Summary of the Language

This Appendix provides a brief summary of the portions of the BASIC language covered in the text. Only the syntax (i.e., what one is allowed to write) is covered here. The semantics (i.e., what the language means) must be found in the text.

The following specifications are applicable for installations using Dartmouth/GE systems and those using the UWBIC system (with the exceptions noted). Nothing here is new; the material is simply repeated for easy reference.

Definitions

Constant   A number written explicitly, or composed of digits with or without a decimal point and/or sign

Line number   An integer number between 1 and 99999 (Dartmouth/GE systems) or between 1 and 9999 (UWBIC systems)

Simple variable $\begin{cases} \text{A single } letter \text{ or} \\ \text{a } letter \text{ followed by a } digit \end{cases}$

Subscripted variable $\begin{cases} Letter \, (expression) \text{ or} \\ letter \, (expression, expression) \end{cases}$

135

Operator
First priority { ↑ Dartmouth/GE systems | ** UWBIC systems } exponentiation

Second priority { * multiplication | / division }

Third priority { + addition | − subtraction }

Expression { A *variable* or a *constant* or any combination of variables and/or constants connected by operators }

Label { " any text " (Dartmouth/GE systems) | ' any text ' (UWBIC systems) }

		Dartmouth/GE systems	UWBIC systems
Comparison	Greater than	>	GT
	Greater than or equal to	> =	GE
	Less than	<	LT
	Less than or equal to	< =	LE
	Not equal to	< >	NE
	Equal to	=	=

Statement Types

REM any text
REMARK any text

READ *variable*
READ *variable, . . . , variable*

LET *variable* = *expression*
GO TO *line number*

IF *expression   comparison   expression*   THEN *line number*

FOR *simple variable* = *expression* TO *expression* STEP *expression*
FOR *simple variable* = *expression* TO *expression*
NEXT *simple variable*

GOSUB *line number*
RETURN

PRINT
PRINT *expression*
PRINT *label*

$$\text{PRINT} \left\{ \begin{matrix} label \\ \text{or} \\ expression \end{matrix} \right\} , \ldots , \left\{ \begin{matrix} label \\ \text{or} \\ expression \end{matrix} \right\} \left\{ \begin{matrix} , \\ \text{or} \\ blank \end{matrix} \right\}$$

DIM *letter* (*integer constant*)
DIM *letter* (*integer constant, integer constant*)

DATA *constant*
DATA *constant* , . . . , *constant*

STOP

functions

LOG	Natural logarithm
EXP	Exponential
ABS	Absolute value
SQR	Square root
INT	Integer part
SIN	Sine
COS	Cosine
TAN	Tangent
ATN	Arctangent
RND	Random number

Definitions

Constant   A number written explicitly, or composed of digits with or without a decimal point and/or sign

Line number   An integer number between 1 and 99999 (Dartmouth/GE systems) or between 1 and 9999 (UWBIC systems)

Simple variable $\begin{cases} \text{A } \textit{single letter} \text{ or} \\ \text{a } \textit{letter} \text{ followed by a } \textit{digit} \end{cases}$

Subscripted variable $\begin{cases} \textit{Letter (expression)} \text{ or} \\ \textit{letter (expression, expression)} \end{cases}$

Operator $\begin{cases} \text{First priority} & \begin{cases} \uparrow \text{ Dartmouth/GE systems} \\ ** \text{ UWBIC systems} \end{cases} \} \text{ exponentiation} \\ \text{Second priority} & \begin{cases} * \text{ multiplication} \\ / \text{ division} \end{cases} \\ \text{Third priority} & \begin{cases} + \text{ addition} \\ - \text{ subtraction} \end{cases} \end{cases}$

Expression $\begin{cases} \text{A } \textit{variable} \text{ or} \\ \text{a } \textit{constant} \text{ or} \\ \text{any combination of variables and/or constants connected} \\ \text{by operators} \end{cases}$

Label $\begin{cases} \texttt{"} \text{ any text } \texttt{"} \text{ (Dartmouth/GE systems)} \\ \texttt{'} \text{ any text } \texttt{'} \text{ (UWBIC systems)} \end{cases}$

		Dartmouth/GE systems	UWBIC systems
Comparison	Greater than	>	GT
	Greater than or equal to	>=	GE
	Less than	<	LT
	Less than or equal to	<=	LE
	Not equal to	<>	NE
	Equal to	=	=